ALASKA GEOGRAF

Volume 19, Number 2

ALASKA:
The Great Land

The Alaska Geographic Society

To teach many more to better know and more wisely use our natural resources

EDITOR
Penny Rennick

PRODUCTION DIRECTOR
Kathy Doogan

STAFF WRITER
L.J. Campbell

MARKETING MANAGER
Jan Westfall

CIRCULATION/DATABASE MANAGER
Kevin Kerns

POSTMASTER: Send address changes to
ALASKA GEOGRAPHIC®
P.O. Box 93370
Anchorage, Alaska 99509-3370

COVER: *Fireweed and rapeseed brighten this view of the lush Matanuska Valley in southcentral Alaska. Long one of the state's main agricultural areas, Mat Valley agriculture got a boost in 1935 when the federal government brought 200 families from the northern Midwest to farm the area under the Matanuska Valley Colonization Project, a Great Depression relief effort. (John W. Warden)*

PREVIOUS PAGE: *A Swiss hiker enjoys an unparalleled view high above the Kongakut River valley in the Arctic National Wildlife Refuge of extreme northeastern Alaska. (Chlaus Lotscher)*

FACING PAGE: *Capt. Frederick W. Beechey noted in 1826 that the horned puffin was one of the most abundant Alaskan seabirds, when he described a steep rock near Chamisso Island in Kotzebue Sound that he called Puffin Island. (David G. Roseneau)*

ALASKA GEOGRAPHIC® (ISSN 0361-1353) is published quarterly by The Alaska Geographic Society, 639 West International, Unit 38, Anchorage, AK 99518. Second-class postage paid at Anchorage, Alaska, and additional mailing offices. Printed in U.S.A. Copyright © 1992 by The Alaska Geographic Society. All rights reserved. Registered trademark: Alaska Geographic, ISSN 0361-1353; Key title Alaska Geographic.

THE ALASKA GEOGRAPHIC SOCIETY is a non-profit organization exploring new frontiers of knowledge across the lands of the Polar Rim, putting the geography book back in the classroom, exploring new methods of teaching and learning—sharing in the excitement of discovery in man's wonderful new world north of 51°16'.

SOCIETY MEMBERS receive *ALASKA GEOGRAPHIC*®, a quality magazine that devotes each quarterly issue to monographic in-depth coverage of a northern geographic region or resource-oriented subject.

MEMBERSHIP in The Alaska Geographic Society costs $39 per year, $49 to non-U.S. addresses. ($31.20 of the $39 is for a one-year subscription to *ALASKA GEOGRAPHIC*®.) Order from The Alaska Geographic Society, P.O. Box 93370, Anchorage, AK 99509-3370; phone (907) 562-0164, FAX (907) 562-0479.

SUBMITTING PHOTOGRAPHS: Please write for a list of upcoming topics or other specific photo needs and a copy of our editorial guidelines. We cannot be responsible for unsolicited submissions. Submissions not accompanied by sufficient postage for return by certified mail will be returned by regular mail.

CHANGE OF ADDRESS: The post office does not automatically forward *ALASKA GEOGRAPHIC*® when you move. To ensure continuous service, please notify us six weeks before moving. Send your new address, and, if possible, your membership number or a mailing label from a recent *ALASKA GEOGRAPHIC*® to: The Alaska Geographic Society, P.O. Box 93370, Anchorage, AK 99509-3370.

MAILING LISTS: We occasionally make our members' names and addresses available to carefully screened publications and companies whose products and activities may be of interest to you. If you prefer not to receive such mailings, please advise us, and include your mailing label (or your name and address if label is not available).

ABOUT THIS ISSUE: Time after time readers of the *ALASKA GEOGRAPHIC*® series have asked for an issue that takes in the entire state, giving the basics of each region with lots of photos. Well, here it is. Alaska Geographic staff prepared the main text, with smaller articles on a few of the individuals who have contributed to Alaska's reputation as the Great Land. Freelance writer and former U.S. Geological Survey scientist Richard Emanuel prepared the material on John Mertie, who knew the Great Land more intimately than most. Chris Wooley and staff of the Inupiat History, Language and Culture Commission share with readers the photographs of Marvin Peter, who captured the Eskimo lifestyle with his camera. Stuart Pechek brings readers into his remote cabin in the Interior from which he traps each winter among the solitary forests on the south side of the Brooks Range.

Thanks to all the photographers who shared some of their favorite images of the Great Land. We welcome you all to take this look at Alaska, The Great Land.

COLOR SEPARATIONS BY: Graphic Chromatics

PRINTED BY: Hart Press

PRICE TO NON-MEMBERS THIS ISSUE: $18.95

ISBN: 1-56661-002-8 (paper);
1-56661-003-6 (hardback)

CONTENTS

INTRODUCTION

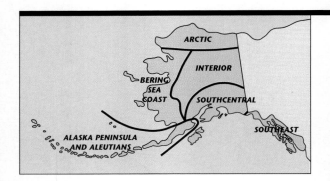

IN THE EXTREME NORTHWESTERN corner of North America sits a land that the Aleuts called Alyeska. At 586,412 square miles, Alaska's claim to greatness is more than just talk. It is the nation's biggest state. It has the continent's highest mountain, the longest shoreline of any state, glaciers as large as the entire state of Rhode Island. Alaska's borders contain the country's northernmost, westernmost and, depending on perspective, easternmost points. But Alaska is more than just big, it is also bold: massive ice fields, towering forests, seemingly endless tundra-covered plains, shifting sand dunes above the Arctic Circle and one of the largest river deltas on the west coast of the Western Hemisphere.

It is a land where, as Barry Lopez writes in *Arctic Dreams* (1986), "polar bears fall down out of the skies" and dreams flourish before the nest of a horned lark. Alaska has had more than its share of larks. Take Slim Rydeen who set off on snowshoes from Candle on the Seward Peninsula to walk to the Gulf of Alaska from where he caught a boat for Juneau to attend the Territorial Legislature. Take the gold seekers who skated or bicycled down the ice of the Yukon River heading from the rush at Dawson City to the one at Nome. Or Roald Amundsen who walked from the arctic coast across the Brooks Range to Eagle on the Yukon to telegraph news of his successful traverse of the Northwest Passage. Or the Italian Duke of Abruzzi who in 1897 made the first successful ascent of Mount St. Elias, the continent's third highest peak, only to find that about 30 miles away stood another even higher.

These explorers and adventurers of the last hundred years carry on the traditions of the explorers of the 18th century, in particular the Russians who set out on the great eastern sea. In their landfalls on the new continent, they encountered descendants of perhaps some of the greatest wanderers of all time. They came upon Aleuts and Tlingits, whose aboriginal ancestors unknowingly peopled a hemisphere. From these traditions has come the mystique of a great north land. Its land, its animals and its people have melded into what Alaskans call the Great Land.

The season's first snowfall, known to Alaskans as termination dust because it signals the approaching end of summer, frosts hills near Broad Pass on Labor Day weekend. (George Matz)

Akhiok **I8**
Akiak **G6**
Akutan **F9**
Alakanuk **F5**
Aleknagik **H7**
Allakaket **I3**
Ambler **H3**
Anadyr (Russia) **B4**
Anaktuvuk Pass **J2**
Anchorage **J6**
Anderson **J4**
Angoon **N8**
Aniak **H6**
Anvik **G5**
Arctic Village **K2**
Atka **D10**
Atmautluak **G6**
Atqasuk **H1**
Barrow **H1**
Bethel **G6**
Bettles **J3**
Brevig Mission **F4**
Buckland **G4**
Carcross (Canada) **N6**
Carmacks (Canada) **M6**
Chefornak **C6**
Chevak **F6**
Chignik **H8**
Chuathbaluk **H6**
Circle **K4**
Clark's Point **H7**
Coffman Cove **N8**
Cold Bay **G9**
Cordova **K6**
Craig **N9**
Dawson City (Canada) **M5**
Deering **G4**
Delta Junction **K4**
Dillingham **H7**
Diomede **E4**
Eagle **L4**
Eek **G6**
Ekwok **H7**
Elim **G4**
Emmonak **F5**
Fairbanks **K4**
False Pass **G9**
Fort McPherson (Canada) **N3**
Fort Yukon **K3**
Galena **H4**
Gambell **E5**
Golovin **G4**
Goodnews Bay **G7**
Grayling **H5**

Haines **N7**
Haines Junction (Canada) **M6**
Holy Cross **H5**
Homer **J7**
Hoonah **N7**
Hooper Bay **F6**
Houston **J6**
Hughes **I4**
Huslia **I4**
Hydaburg **N9**
Hyder **O8**
Inuvik (Canada) **N2**
Juneau **N7**
Kachemak **J7**
Kake **N8**
Kaktovik **L2**
Kaltag **H4**
Kasaan **N9**
Kasigluk **G6**
Kenai **J6**
Ketchikan **N9**
Kiana **G3**
King Cove **G9**
Kivalina **F3**
Klawock **N8**
Kobuk **I3**
Kodiak **I8**
Kotlik **G5**
Kotzebue **G3**
Koyuk **G4**
Koyukuk **H4**
Kupreanof **N8**
Kwethluk **G6**
Larsen Bay **I8**
Lavrentiya (Russia) **E4**
Lower Kalskag **G6**
Manokotak **H7**
Marshall **G5**
McCarthy **L6**
McGrath **I5**
Mekoryuk **F6**
Metlakatla **O9**
Mountain Village **G5**
Napakiak **G6**
Napaskiak **G6**
Nenana **J4**
New Stuyahok **H7**
Newhalen **I7**
Newtok **F6**
Nightmute **F6**
Nikolai **I5**
Nome **F4**
Nondalton **I6**
Noorvik **G3**

North Pole **K4**
Nuiqsut **J1**
Nulato **H4**
Nunapitchuk **G6**
Old Harbor **I8**
Ouzinkie **I8**
Palmer **J6**
Pelican **M7**
Petersburg **N8**
Pilot Point **H8**
Pilot Station **G5**
Platinum **G7**
Point Hope **F2**
Point Lay **I2**
Port Heiden **H8**
Port Lions **I8**
Port Alexander **N8**
Provideniya (Russia) **D4**
Prudhoe Bay **J2**
Quinhagak **G7**
Ross River (Canada) **N6**
Ruby **I4**
Russian Mission **G6**
Saint George **E8**
Saint Mary's **G5**
Saint Michael **G5**
Saint Paul **E8**
Sand Point **H9**
Savoonga **E5**
Saxman **O9**
Scammon Bay **F5**
Selawik **H3**
Seldovia **J7**
Seward **J6**
Shageluk **H5**
Shaktoolik **G4**
Sheldon Point **F5**
Shishmaref **F4**
Shungnak **H3**
Sitka **N8**
Skagway **N7**
Soldotna **J6**
Stebbins **G5**
Tanana **J4**
Teller **F4**
Tenakee Springs **N7**
Thorne Bay **N8**
Tofty **J4**
Togiak **H7**
Toksook Bay **F6**
Tuluksak **G6**
Tununak **F6**
Uelen (Russia) **E4**
Umiat **I2**

Unalakleet **G5**
Unalaska **F10**
Upper Kalskag **H6**
Valdez **K6**
Venetie **K3**
Wainwright **H1**
Wales **F4**
Wasilla **J6**
Watson Lake (Canada) **O6**
Whitehorse (Canada) **N6**
White Mountain **G4**
Whittier **J6**
Wrangell **N8**
Yakutat **M7**

HIGHWAYS
  1 Alaska Highway
  2 Cassiar Highway
  3 Klondike Highway 2
  4 Haines Highway
  5 Campbell Highway
  6 Canol Road
  7 Klondike Loop
  8 Dempster Highway
  9 Richardson Highway
10 Glenn Highway
11 Seward Highway
12 Sterling Highway
13 George Parks Highway
14 Denali Highway
15 Edgerton Highway
16 Taylor Highway
17 Steese Highway
18 Dalton Highway
19 Elliott Highway

ALASKA:
The Great Land

(ALASKA GEOGRAPHIC® map by Kathy Doogan)

0   100   200
MILES

ATTU ISLAND

ALEUTIAN ISLANDS

KISKA ISLAND

AMCHITKA ISLAND

ADAK ISLAND

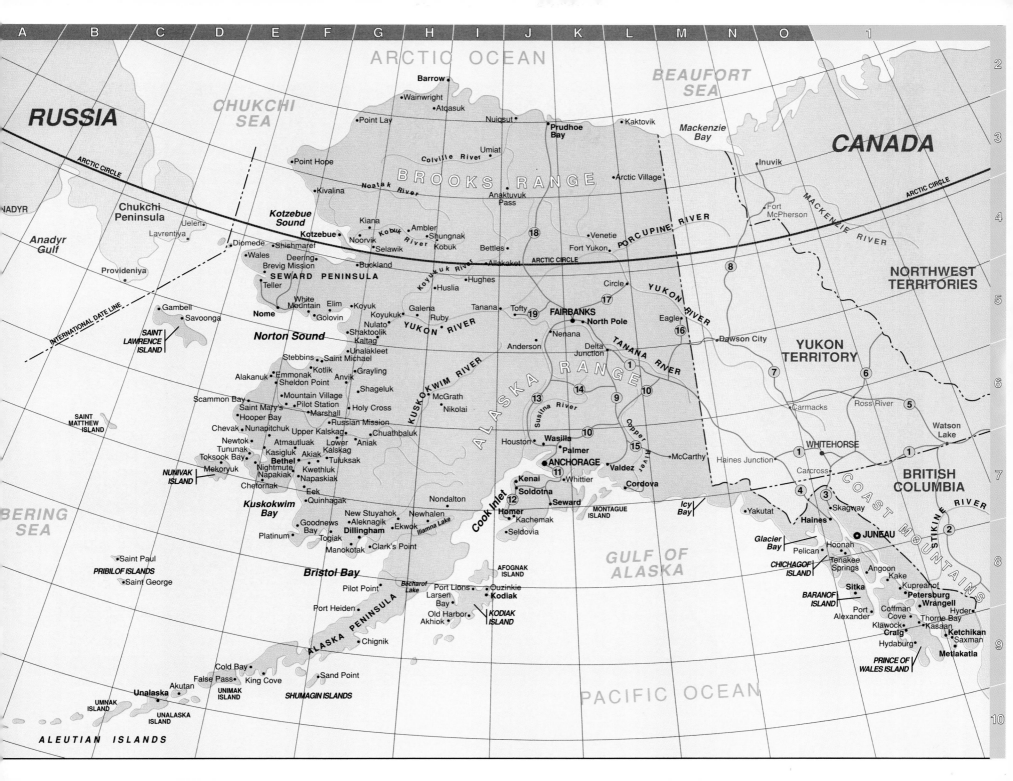

LEFT: *Certainly part of the Great Land's mystique is the aurora borealis or northern lights. (Cary Anderson)*

BELOW: *The bright orange bill and bright eye make the oystercatcher unmistakable. This species forages along Alaska's coast from Southeast to the Aleutians. (John Hyde)*

RIGHT: *When Westerners first arrived in Southeast, they encountered tribes of Tlingit Indians, and smaller bands of Haidas. Among the most powerful Tlingits were those of Klukwan, a village on the Chilkat River near Haines. Joe Hotch, Sr., head of the Eagle Clan, wears traditional regalia at Klukwan. (Roy M. Corral)*

Alaska's Panhandle:
SOUTHEAST

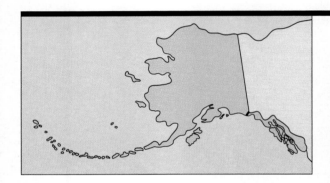

FROM DIXON ENTRANCE 560 MILES north to Icy Bay lies a sliver of mainland and a string of islands that sustain fishing, forestry, government and tourism. This is southeastern Alaska, typically referred to as Southeast or the Panhandle. At its widest point on a diameter from Dall Island to a crook in the border with Canada north of Hyder, the region stretches a mere 143 miles.

In Southeast, travel frequently requires a boat or plane. Forested mountaintops surrounded by water, and narrow fiords and valleys filled with ice hinder road construction. Although the road system is expanding a bit — mostly in support of logging and chiefly on Prince of Wales Island — there still are not many miles. Schemers and dreamers have talked about calling nature's bluff, blasting a road up Taku Inlet or bridging Lynn Canal, for instance. But the terrain has so far proven insurmountable. Only a gravel spur off Canada's Cassiar Highway into tiny Hyder, and the Klondike Highway 2 into Skagway or Haines Highway into Haines, connect Southeast to the continental highway network. And when the winds howl, the boats do not sail; and when the fog settles, the planes do not fly. Isolation remains a characteristic of Southeast.

Weather is one thing Southeast has plenty of: rain, wind, snow and more rain. Moderated by its maritime environment, Southeast's winter temperatures are frequently higher than the rest of the state. Metlakatla, south of Ketchikan, tops Alaska's winter readings many a day. In Juneau, winter tempertures average about 27 degrees. Summer recordings, however, are likely to be lower than other areas of the state. For Juneau the average is about 54 degrees. The region is known for its rain. Ketchikan proudly acknowledges its abundant rainfall with a liquid sunshine gauge. Not surprisingly, all that rain in summer can turn to snow in winter, with Yakutat on Yakutat Bay receiving an average of 17 plus feet annually. Southeast has wind, too. Taku winds they are sometimes called. They sweep off the glaciers and howl down out of

One of the houses of the waterfront community of Kupreanof, formerly West Petersburg, sparkles in the sunshine on Kupreanof Island's Lindenberg Peninsula. Wrangell Narrows separates the peninsula from Mitkof Island, location of Petersburg. (Don Pitcher)

FACING PAGE: *Visitors scatter throughout downtown Juneau, while a cruise ship ties up at a dock along Gastineau Channel. Tourism is one of the major industries in Southeast, where many visitors arrive by cruise ships and ferries. In summer 1990, more than 31,000 passengers arrived in Juneau by cruise ship. (Dean Abramson)*

RIGHT: *Largest of the world's swans, trumpeters routinely weigh 25 to 35 pounds, and occasionally reach 40 pounds. Eighty percent of this species nests in Alaska, where they can be seen in winter at Blind Slough near Petersburg. (Shelley Schneider)*

the mountains. Winds scouring the Stikine River's large delta sometimes create bands of dust and silt in the air that are visible from Wrangell, several miles to the south.

Mountains and glaciers, Southeast has plenty of those also. Pleistocene ice sheets shaped much of the region. When they retreated 10,000 to 15,000 years ago, they left behind mountains; sheer, scoured peaks; U-shaped valleys and twisting fiords. When the ice sheets melted, sea level rose, surrounding the mountaintops, filling the valleys, creating the basic Southeast landscape of today. The spine of the Coast Mountains borders the region on the east. As these mountains pass Skagway, they join with the Fairweather Range and the St. Elias Mountains and crowd the coast. The St. Elias is the highest coastal barrier range in the world, and backs one of the world's truly immense wildernesses.

There is no lack of glaciers in Southeast either, from LeConte, southernmost tidewater glacier on the continent, to the massive piedmont lobe of Malaspina, itself larger than Rhode Island.

In recent years, scientists have gathered near the head of Yakutat Bay to study the movements of Hubbard Glacier, longest tidewater glacier in North America with a total length, including its Canadian source, of 76 miles. Hubbard has threatened to advance and seal the mouth of Russell Fiord. Between November 1985 and May 1986 the glacier pushed forward, depositing a dam of ice and mud

BELOW: *Logging is an important industry in Southeast, where substantial patches of clearcutting are noticeable, particularly on northern Prince of Wales Island. Here choker setters Jay Schnider and Brian Heersink prepare to attach cable to logs in a clearcut near Klawock on Prince of Wales Island. When they give the signal, a yarder will winch the logs to a landing where they will be loaded onto trucks. (Walt Matell)*

ABOVE: *Much of Southeast's tree-covered terrain lies within Tongass National Forest, the nation's largest. Beneath the rainforest's canopy grow such plants as horsetails (foreground), bracken ferns, bunchberries and devil's club (upper right). (Rex Melton)*

at the mouth of Russell Fiord, and turning the fiord into a lake. The level of the lake rose to 82 feet, prompting concern that it might overflow into the nearby Situk River, ruining a major subsistence and sport fishery. On October 8, 1986, the dam suddenly gave way, draining the lake into Disenchantment Bay at the head of Yakutat Bay. According to U.S. Geological Survey scientists, the lake drained at about 3.7 million cubic feet per second, and returned to sea level within two days. This was only a

Known for its spectacular setting, the City and Borough of Sitka, population 8,588, encompasses almost 8,000 square miles of Baranof Island. Alexander Baranof, chief manager of the Russian-American Co., opened a post here in 1799. Tlingits attacked his post in June 1802; in 1804 Baranof returned with reinforcements and subdued the Natives. The Russians renewed their efforts to set up a post, establishing New Archangel on the present site of Sitka. Around the post grew the community that eventually became the capital of Russian America. (Rex Melton)

FACING PAGE: *Totems confirm the Tlingit Indian history of Klawock, on Klawock Inlet on the west coast of Prince of Wales Island. The community of 758 began in 1868 as a trading post, salmon saltery and fishing village. The first salmon cannery in Alaska was opened here a decade later. (Don Pitcher)*

RIGHT: *The coastal rainforest surrounds Heckman Lake near Ketchikan. Most of the state's commercial timber grows within the dense coastal forests of southern Alaska. In Southeast, western hemlock and Sitka spruce predominate, with smaller stands of mountain hemlock, western redcedar and Alaska-cedar. (Don Pitcher)*

BOTTOM RIGHT: *The LeConte glacier, southernmost active tidewater glacier in North America, enters LeConte Bay and Frederick Sound just north of the Stikine River delta. The glacier was named for Joseph LeConte, professor of geology at the University of California. (Rex Melton)*

temporary reprieve, however, because the following year Hubbard again advanced and overrode Osier Island at the entrance to the fiord. The glacier has not yet completely blocked the entrance, but scientists seem confident that it is only a matter of time.

Perhaps the most visited remnant of the Pleistocene ice blanket is Glacier Bay National Park and Preserve. The park's glaciers advance and retreat as they are fed by incoming snowfall. At Park Headquarters in Bartlett Cove, an average of 75 inches of rain and 120 inches of snow fall each year. Two hundred years ago, when British Capt. James Cook sailed along this coast, the ice reached well out into Icy Strait and the bay did not exist. Since then, the ice has retreated enough to expose two long fingers and several stubby ones that stretch inland to the glaciers' faces.

In the early 1990s, Glacier Bay's rivers of ice on the whole are no longer retreating at the pace that produced the bay. Most have stabilized or are holding their own, with a few exceptions such as McBride and Casement.

LEFT: *The Stikine River, here shown 20 miles from its mouth in U.S. territory, drains 20,000 square miles of northwestern British Columbia and a bit of the Coast Mountains north of Wrangell. The Stikine is the largest river entering Southeast waters.* (Rex Melton)

FACING PAGE: *A hiker overlooks Gastineau Channel, Douglas Island across the water, and downtown Juneau, Alaska's capitol. The bridge from Juneau across to smaller Douglas was opened in 1981, replacing an earlier span christened in 1935.* (Skip Gray)

More retreat is being detected in the land-locked glaciers; in general the tidal glaciers, such as Grand Pacific and Johns Hopkins, have stabilized or are advancing.

From some of the glaciers flow rivers, and although they are not as important in Southeast as elsewhere in Alaska, still the region has some noteworthy streams. At Dry Bay, south of Yakutat, the Alsek, having picked up water from the Tatshenshini, enters the Gulf of Alaska. Wild rivers both, only in recent decades have stretches of these rivers been routinely navigated.

The Chilkat River near Haines is best known for its eagles that congregate in the Chilkat Bald Eagle Preserve each fall to feed on a late run of chum salmon.

The region's premier river, the Stikine, enters saltwater a few miles from Wrangell. Because it breaks through the coastal mountain barrier from its source high on the Spatsizi Plateau of British Columbia, the Stikine has been an important commercial corridor since the days when furs and gold were hauled along the river. For more than a century paddlewheelers and smaller craft have taken on passengers and supplies in Wrangell for the run upriver.

Southeast's moist environment provides suitable habitat for the Pacific Coast temperate rainforest to extend north into Alaska. Most of it is included within Tongass National Forest, the nation's largest at 16.8 million acres. Western hemlock and Sitka spruce make up about 90 percent of the forest, with smaller stands of western redcedar, Alaska-cedar, mountain hemlock and numerous other species.

Within the forests live brown and black bear, Sitka black-tailed deer, moose, wolves and smaller furbearers. In the Yakutat area is found a color phase of the black bear known as the glacier or blue bear.

Alaska Department of Fish and Game staff transplanted 50 elk to Etolin Island in 1987. The elk did not do well initially, but recently have increased their numbers to between 50 and 100 animals. Part of the group has swum to neighboring Zarembo Island to establish a second herd. A smaller group has crossed to Brownson Island, a small island that is connected to Etolin at low tide.

On extremely rocky slopes above the fiords live mountain goats. In 1990, a cougar was shot near Wrangell,

in what was the first confirmed sighting of this species on Southeast's islands.

Beneath the mountains and glaciers lie extensive mineral deposits. In the heart of Misty Fiords National Monument, an area surrounding a major molybdenum deposit has been set aside for possible future development. U.S. Borax did substantial preliminary work on its Quartz Hill project, but low worldwide molybdenum prices have halted development for the moment. In the meantime, U.S. Borax sold Quartz Hill to Cominco, the mining conglomerate that also controls the giant Red Dog Mine in northwestern Alaska.

At Greens Creek above Hawk Inlet on northern Admiralty Island, Kennecott, the North American subsidiary of a worldwide mining consortium, operates the Greens Creek Mine, a silver, gold, zinc and lead producer. In 1991 Greens Creek mined 7.6 million ounces of silver, making it the nation's largest producer.

Other major mineral deposits are found in association with the Juneau Gold Belt that stretches more than 100 miles from Windham Bay, 60 miles southeast of Juneau to Berners Bay, about 50 miles to the northwest. Several historic mines worked gold from this band of mineralization. The Treadwell and A-J (Alaska Juneau) mines were

FACING PAGE: *Gulls soar above Adams Inlet in Glacier Bay National Park. When glaciers first begin to retreat, they leave behind moraines and gravel bars. These newly exposed terrains are the first to be colonized by plants in their effort to revegetate lands scoured bare by the glacier. (Shelley Schneider)*

RIGHT: *A shrimp trawler plies waters off the Elephant's Nose, the northern tip of Woronkofski Island west of Wrangell. (Rex Melton)*

BOTTOM RIGHT: *Garnet Ledge Creek tumbles near an area in the Stikine Valley with exposed garnet ledges. Fred Hanford, a former mayor of Wrangell, deeded his claim to a garnet ledge in this area in 1962 to the Boy Scouts and children of Wrangell. Today the claim is mined by youngsters who sell the garnets to passengers coming off the ferries and cruise ships at Wrangell. (Joey Barnes)*

once world famous, fueling much of Juneau and Douglas' economy. Echo Bay Mines Ltd. is hoping new technology and increased gold prices will enable them to reopen the A-J. Developers are also looking to resurrect the Jualin and Kensington mines near Berners Bay.

All of Southeast's main communities and most of its settlements are located along the coast. They got their start here as fur trading posts, gold mining camps, fishing ports and cannery sites or as missions. About 90 percent of the region's population lives in Juneau, Ketchikan, Sitka, Petersburg, Wrangell, Craig, Haines and Skagway. Most smaller settlements revolve around logging, fishing or tourism. Some are floating logging camps, or tiny canneries around which are clustered a few houses. Most of the smaller settlements provide the simple basics of daily living, but any services out of the ordinary, like specialized dentistry for instance, necessitate travel to Juneau or Ketchikan. For the most part, however, residents of Southeast are resourceful. There is always fish to eat, berries to pick, wood for fires and boughs for shelter. Southeast is a rich land. The Natives who settled Southeast, the Tlingits, Haidas and Tsimshians, knew this and thrived; today's residents are just as perceptive.

Urbanism on the Last Frontier:
SOUTHCENTRAL

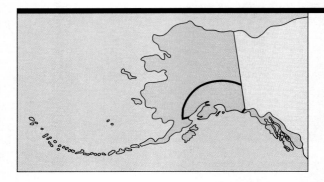

SOUTHCENTRAL ALASKA EXTENDS from Icy Bay west to the south side of Lake Iliamna and north to the crest of the Alaska Range. A glance at the region around Icy Bay gives the impression that Southcentral is ruled by the same glaciers that dominate Southeast. But except for the southeastern corner and the mountain heights that rim the region's basin, Southcentral offers more varied terrain than Southeast and its glaciers seem less obvious.

Basically Southcentral is shaped like an inverted gravy boat, rimmed by mountains and open to the Gulf of Alaska through its pouring spout down 220-mile-long Cook Inlet. The handle of the gravy boat is lost in the jumble of the Wrangell and St. Elias mountains at the southeast corner. The Kodiak archipelago dribbles from the spout into the west side of the Gulf of Alaska. It is approximately 650 miles across the gulf from Sitka to the town of Kodiak.

The other major indentation in Southcentral's coastline is Prince William Sound. Recreationists value the sound for its numerous passages and islands to explore. Fishing fleets cruise the waterway for salmon, herring and shellfish. And giant tankers carry North Slope oil from the southern terminus of the trans-Alaska pipeline at Valdez through the sound to ports beyond Alaska. The tanker *Exxon Valdez* got hung up on Bligh Reef along this route in March 1989, causing an oil spill of about 11 million gallons that soiled much of the coastline in western Prince William Sound and for hundreds of miles west along the Gulf of Alaska.

The Alaska Range is the highest of the mountain barriers bordering Southcentral. Mount McKinley, the continent's tallest peak, tops the lofty range at 20,320 feet. McKinley was remeasured using new techniques in 1989 and found to be 14 feet lower, but as of spring 1992 official National Park Service records still list the traditional elevation. Mount Foraker, Alaska's third highest and North

One of the favored harbors for Southcentral boat owners, Whittier, population 279, lies along the south shore of Passage Canal in Prince William Sound. The town, established during World War II as a personnel and supply transshipment point, is only accessible by boat, plane or rail spur off the Alaska Railroad line at Portage. (Harry M. Walker)

America's fourth highest at 17,400 feet, rises just to the west of McKinley. The Alaska Range blends with the Aleutian Range on the west side of Cook Inlet, and curves to the east to meet the Wrangell and St. Elias mountains. Sitting just inland from Icy Bay in the St. Elias Mountains is Mount St. Elias itself. At 18,008 feet, the peak is the second highest in Alaska and the third highest on the continent. The Chugach Mountains, and Kenai Mountains farther west, protect Southcentral's interior from the full fury of Gulf of Alaska storms. The only major breach in this barrier is the Copper River, a furious torrent that curves down out of the north side of the Wrangell Mountains. The river carries its sediment load past the Copper River Highway east of Cordova and out into the Gulf of Alaska, where the sediment settles out in one of the largest loads deposited by any Alaskan river.

In addition to the Copper, Southcentral has two other major river systems: the Susitna and the Matanuska. The Susitna flows 260 miles from the upper Nelchina Basin, between the Alaska Range and Talkeetna Mountains and south toward Cook Inlet. The Susitna Valley supports abundant wildlife and viable fishing, hunting and trapping industries. The Matanuska River begins about 75 miles east of Anchorage at Matanuska Glacier and runs through a

LEFT: *The center of urban Alaska, Anchorage's 230,000 residents lead a lifestyle typical of much of urban America. This view looking over the Westchester area shows Anchorage's two tallest buildings, the ARCO building on the left and the Enserch Center at right. (John W. Warden)*

FACING PAGE: *Narrow, northeast-southwest-trending fiords characterize much of Prince William Sound's coastline. In the northwest corner of the sound lies Harriman Fiord, which runs 12 miles from Harriman Glacier to Barry Arm. Railroad magnate Edward H. Harriman organized an expedition to explore Alaska's coastline in 1899, and when expedition members reached northwestern Prince William Sound, they named many of the glaciers for U.S. colleges and universities. (George Wuerthner)*

spectacular, confined valley before dumping its waters into Knik Arm of Cook Inlet.

Several rivers drain the Kenai Peninsula, and perhaps none is more important than the Kenai River, a renowned salmon stream that weaves from Kenai Lake 75 miles through the lowlands on the peninsula's west side to enter Cook Inlet at the town of Kenai. Commercial, sport and subsistence fishermen depend on the Kenai fish runs, and overuse in recent years has led to restrictions in some fishing.

Although the mountains protect most of Southcentral from the worst of Gulf of Alaska storms, the region's transitional climate varies from a soggy Kodiak with an average 57 inches of rain, to Thompson Pass outside Valdez with a state record 974 inches of snow, to colder, drier Talkeetna with 32 inches of rainfall. Anchorage temperatures range from an average low of 10 in December to an average high of 55 in July.

Archaeologists are still trying to determine when prehistoric man first entered Southcentral. Best estimates place humans here sometime near the end of the Pleistocene glaciation. Archaeologists have found human skull fragments and teeth dated at 6,000 years old from a site on Kodiak Island. In any event, from these original

BELOW: *Fly fishermen try their touch in one of the Fuller lakes on the Kenai Peninsula. Dolly Varden, grayling and rainbow trout occur in lakes and streams along the Fuller lakes trail system, which climbs into the Chugach Mountains on the north side of the Sterling Highway near the east entrance to the Skilak Loop. (Ron Levy)*

RIGHT: *Commercial and sport fishing are important to Southcentral residents. Prince William Sound fishermen look to pink salmon for the bulk of their catch, and in 1991 landed 32.9 million pinks, discarded an additional 2.7 million and sent another 1.5 million to Russia, according to Alaska Department of Fish and Game records. (Kent Wranic)*

people and later intruders evolved the Eyak of the Copper River delta and coastal area, the Ahtna Athabaskans of the Copper River valley, the Chugach Eskimos of Prince William Sound, the Dena'ina Athabaskans of Cook Inlet country and the Koniags of Kodiak. These people looked to the sea or to the rivers for their survival. They took land mammals when they could.

When the Russians first ventured to Southcentral, they generally stayed to the coast, establishing their first permanent settlement in North America at St. Paul on Kodiak in 1784. Later, other forts were built to support the growing fur trade. The Russians opened Fort St. Nicholas, at the mouth of the Kenai River, in 1791.

The vanguard of Americans into Southcentral came primarily for gold. They pushed inland from the coast, up the river valleys. Small gold strikes at Sunrise and Hope brought prospectors to Turnagain Arm in the 1890s.

Others explored up the Susitna and Matanuska valleys. Most paid scant attention to the small stream flowing into Cook Inlet near where Knik and Turnagain arms meet, a site that would grow in the next half-century to become Alaska's largest urban center.

Seward, Valdez and Cordova, all situated along the coast, were the premier communities in Southcentral around the turn of the century and remained so for some time. Cordova got its start with construction of the Copper River & Northwestern Railway to the Kennicott copper deposits in the Wrangell Mountains. Valdez became a port and jumping off point during the gold rush when desire for an all-American route to the Klondike brought gold-seekers to this fiord in northeastern Prince William Sound. U.S. Army Capt. W.R. Abercrombie was sent to Valdez to open up a military road from the coast up the Copper River valley to the Interior, to Eagle on the Yukon River. With access to the north, Valdez prospered.

Seward was founded in 1902 as the tidewater terminus for the Alaska Central Railroad. Various operators sought to build a rail line north to the Interior, but it was not until the federal government took an interest in the project that construction made much headway. The Alaska Railroad, as the line came to be known, certainly boosted Seward's fortunes, but it also gave life to a tent camp at the mouth of Ship Creek near where Knik and Turnagain arms meet. Residents of the camp eventually settled on the name Anchorage.

But the community did not grow from a tent camp in 1915 to a cosmopolitan center overnight. It took a world war, a giant earthquake and an oil industry to nourish a blossoming urbanism. During World War II, the military chose Anchorage as its headquarters for the Aleutian campaign. The influx of personnel and construction of housing and office buildings nudged Anchorage from a small town into a major city.

Then in 1964 the epicenter of one of the largest earthquakes recorded in North America occurred beneath a fiord in northern Prince William Sound. The quake

One of the nation's largest fishing ports and an important center for Coast Guard operations in the Gulf of Alaska and Bering Sea, Kodiak, population 7,229, lies on the east side of Kodiak Island, largest of an island group in the western Gulf of Alaska. Parts of the archipelago are within the Kodiak National Wildlife Refuge, renowned for its large bears; 11,000 acres of another island, Shuyak, are a state park. (Penny Rennick)

shuffled about 50,000 square miles of Southcentral landscape, lowering some areas seven feet, raising others 38 feet, and pushing still others sideways as much as 25 feet. The quake's effects were most noticeable in Cordova, Valdez and Seward. Uplift left Cordova's docks high and dry. Rich fishing grounds at the mouth of the Copper River were altered. Channels once easily traveled became a nightmare for fishing boats. Fish could no longer negotiate waterfalls to reach spawning areas.

The quake destroyed much of Valdez when it loosened

The tanker Keystone Canyon *takes on a load of North Slope crude oil at the terminal at Valdez. The port in northeastern Prince William Sound is the southern terminus of the trans-Alaska oil pipeline. In March 1989, more than 11 million gallons of oil leaked from a tanker outbound through the sound and soiled hundreds of miles of beaches in the sound and along the Gulf of Alaska coast. The oil industry has subsequently updated its procedures for dealing with large spills. (Cary Anderson)*

the shelf on which the town was built and sent it careening into Port Valdez. The town was subsequently rebuilt about four miles to the west, but its economy was severely disrupted for a number of years.

At Seward the quake triggered fires at fuel storage areas and heavily damaged harbor facilities, thus destroying 90 percent of the town's economy. While the coastal communities did recover eventually, they had lost too much ground to a rapidly growing Anchorage to maintain their place in the region's economy When oil was found

at Prudhoe Bay in 1968 and the oil companies selected Anchorage as their in-state headquarters, the city's future as the state's center of commerce, finance and transportation was assured.

The Kenai Peninsula, the area south of Anchorage between Prince William Sound and Cook Inlet, has grown along with Anchorage. Some of the original settlements have died, but when the Seward Highway to Seward and Sterling Highway to Homer were punched through the mountains in the early 1950s, settlements along the route prospered. Then Richfield Oil Corp. discovered oil near the Swanson River in 1957, fueling the economies of Kenai and Soldotna to the point that the towns grew into the largest population center on the peninsula.

The western side of the peninsula has been developed more rapidly than the eastern side, its relatively flat terrain proving more hospitable to settlement. In addition to Kenai and Soldotna, and Homer on Kachemak Bay, numerous smaller communities and many homesteads line the Sterling Highway, creating a more or less continuous string of human habitation from the community of Sterling in the central peninsula west and south to Homer.

Once at Homer, on Kachemak Bay, boaters have reached the threshold of one of Alaska's favorite summer playgrounds. Kachemak offers fishing, beachcombing, abundant coves and islands to explore, fine lodges and the communities of Seldovia and Halibut Cove to visit. The view of Homer Spit and the bay from the bluffs overlooking Kachemak's north shore is one of Alaska's most spectacular vistas.

In many ways, the peninsula has evolved into a weekend playground for Anchorage residents. Fishing, boating, hiking, wildlife watching, and skiing lure urban Alaskans. Kenai National Wildlife Refuge, set aside to assure habitat for moose and other wildlife, has hiking and canoe trails and good freshwater fishing. Kenai Fjords National Park, Kachemak Bay State Park and Kachemak Bay State Wilderness Park cover much of the peninsula's southern border. The National Park Service has developed the Exit Glacier area near Seward for walk-in tourists. On the Kachemak Bay side, sunny weekends bring a flood of visitors, that is if they can make it by the superb fishing on the peninsula's rivers.

North of Anchorage, a series of small communities line the Glenn and George Parks highways. What was once Alaska's premier agricultural area in the Matanuska (Mat) Valley has given way to housing developments, shopping malls and other construction characteristic of distant suburbs to any large city. In 1992 the Glenn Highway, which leads east from Anchorage to join the Alaska Highway at Tok, is being widened to four lanes to handle increased daily traffic from Palmer and Wasilla into Anchorage.

There still is some agriculture in the Matanuska and lower Susitna valleys, but the state's dreams of food self-sufficiency have been thwarted. Alaska's long, summer daylight has produced some giant vegetables, but overall the weather, the cold soils and the state's location on the

This aerial of downtown Cordova, a fishing port of 2,504, shows the boat harbor and industrial waterfront. To the north (top of photo) is Shepherd Point and the entrance to Nelson Bay in eastern Prince William Sound. (Ruth Fairall)

planet have hindered growth of a thriving agricultural industry, despite infusions of money and state-funded agricultural projects. Some Alaskans, especially those living in the Bush, feed themselves largely by subsistence; many others hunt, fish, garden and pick berries and wild edibles to supplement store-bought stocks. And of those groceries that do make their way into Alaska's stores, by far the majority are shipped in from outside the state.

In recent years, outlying communities have grown up in the lower Susitna Valley, forming a suburban Bush. Frozen rivers become snow machine highways in winter; in summer, rivers support boat traffic of year-round residents and urbanites who visit their cabins. Most commerce centers around Skwentna, with homesteads and lodges scattered along the abundant waterways.

With a few exceptions, the west side of Cook Inlet has remained a wilderness. The Indian community of Tyonek, the power plant at Beluga, the oil terminal at Drift River and a few lodges are about it as far as noticeable human activities go. In its wildness, the west side presents a landscape of mountains, many topped with glaciers or permanent snowfields, from which flow rivers through forests of spruce and deciduous trees to the coast.

There are mineral resources on the west side, most notably huge deposits of subbituminous coal west of Tyonek. Developers hope to use open pit mines to extract an estimated 1-billion-ton resource, with 700 million tons of proven reserves. According to plans, it would take at least 30 years and probably much longer to fully exploit this deposit of subbituminous coal, a type of coal used primarily to generate steam in electric power plants. A secondary use for subbituminous is as clinker in rotary kilns that turn limestone into cement. Projections call for the Beluga coal to be shipped out of Alaska, with the majority going to Japan, Korea, Taiwan, Mexico and perhaps some to the Seattle area and to Hawaii.

Volcanoes, three of which have spewed ash over the Cook Inlet basin in recent decades, are about the

LEFT: *Two kayakers rig their collapsible kayak at Halibut Cove, a popular starting point for kayaking in Kachemak Bay. The settlement began as a herring fishing center, and now draws artists, retirees and summer and weekend vacationers. (Charlie Crangle)*

FACING PAGE: *Sixth largest of Alaska's lakes, Lake Clark is 42 miles long, 1 to 4 miles wide and covers 110 square miles. The lake forms the heart of Lake Clark National Park and Preserve, an area of glacier-shaved peaks, alpine lakes, volcanoes, wildlife and few humans. Access is usually by plane through Lake Clark Pass southwest of Anchorage in the Aleutian Range to Port Alsworth or Nondalton. (Dennis Hellawell)*

The Chugach Mountains glow in a winter sunrise near Mile 90 of the Glenn Highway. The Glenn, named for Capt. E.F. Glenn who surveyed the area between Knik Arm and the Copper River valley in 1898, runs from Anchorage to Glennallen, then follows the route of the Tok Cutoff to Tok on the Alaska Highway. Built during World War II, the Glenn is the most direct route for residents of Southcentral to reach the Alaska Highway. (Hugh B. White)

biggest influence on the west side landscape.

From Mount Spurr, across Cook Inlet from Anchorage, a string of volcanoes runs down the spine of the Aleutian Range to the Aleutian Islands. This tumultuous region is part of Alaska's link in the Ring of Fire. On a clear day, residents of Anchorage's Hillside area on the east side of town can look out their windows at Mount Spurr, Mount Redoubt and even Mount Iliamna, active volcanoes all.

Just out of sight is the summit of Mount Augustine, an island volcano in lower Cook Inlet.

Mount Augustine most recently erupted ash in 1986. In late 1989 and early 1990, ash from a Redoubt eruption closed Anchorage International Airport. Anchorage received a previous good dusting of ash in 1953 from Mount Spurr.

Volcanic eruptions through time contributed significantly to the profile of Kodiak Island. During the past 8,000 years, blasts of ash from nearby volcanoes have doused the land, adding layers of soil material to what otherwise would have been bare rock, according to archaeologist Rick Knecht. The most recent evidence of this followed the June 1912 eruption of Novarupta volcano, located 100 miles to the west on the Alaska Peninsula. The ash on Kodiak measured 18 inches deep on level ground, considerably deeper in some areas filling streams and lakes. Though damage at the time was considerable, two years later the land was supporting lush grasses and berries.

Kodiak Island and 15 nearby islands form an archipelago on the western edge of the Gulf of Alaska, 50 miles south of the southern tip of the Kenai Peninsula and 30 miles across Shelikof Strait from the Alaska Peninsula. Mountains on the islands range from 2,000 feet to 3,500 feet, with few peaks more than 4,000 feet high. Most of the region's coastline is intricately outlined by deep, narrow, glacier-scoured straits and fiords.

Kodiak Island, at more than 3,500 square miles, is the largest and most populated of the group. The City of Kodiak, with its busy fishing port and numerous seafood processors, is headquarters to the western Gulf of Alaska crab, salmon and bottomfish fleets. While fishing predominates, logging of Native land claims on Afognak Island also contributes to the economy. The city anticipates some growth in tourism, particularly small cruise boats catering to adventure seekers.

Kodiak served as the first capital for Russian America, before the center of Russian government was moved to

Sitka in 1794, and continued as a major commercial center until the sale of Alaska to the United States in 1867. The town existed as an isolated, small fishing village until 1939, when wartime brought troops to the island. With the opening of a U.S. Naval Air Station, the population boomed with more than 20,000 people. In 1972, the U.S. Coast Guard took control of former Navy facilities and today, the Coast Guard Support Center Kodiak is the largest operation base in the service.

Native villages on Kodiak Island include Old Harbor, Akhiok, Karluk and Larsen Bay. Port Lions, the newest settlement on Kodiak Island, was built following the 1964 earthquake for Afognak islanders displaced by the destruction of their village. The archipelago's only other community is Ouzinkie on tiny Spruce Island.

This mixture of urban, suburban and rural; and of modern commerce and traditional subsistence has made Southcentral the anchor for other regions to the north and west. Tourists, trends, technologies and trinkets find their way into Alaska through Southcentral. Many travel north beyond the Alaska Range and enter the great Interior.

LEFT: *The Susitna Valley is another recreation area for Southcentral residents. Numerous good fishing streams flow through the area, hunters go for moose in fall and trappers search for furbearers in winter. Just south of Denali National Park lies Denali State Park, a popular fishing and hiking area. This floatplane has landed on one of the lakes in the park with Mount McKinley as a backdrop. (Steve McCutcheon)*

ABOVE: *Anchorage residents are fortunate to have varied wildlife close to their urban center. Moose are common in residential areas, especially in winter. The city is the largest urban center in the nation to have nesting loons, and bears and other wildlife inhabit the Chugach Mountains on the edge of town. One of three ptarmigan species found in the state, this white-tailed ptarmigan and its chicks nested high in the Chugach. (Charlie Crangle)*

John Beaver Mertie Jr.

By Richard P. Emanuel

Editor's note: *Geologist John Beaver Mertie appreciated the Great Land more than most. A freelance writer and former hydrologist with the U.S. Geological Survey, Richard P. Emanuel, who specializes in science topics, has prepared this glance at Mertie's many adventures in Alaska.*

In 1911, in his hometown of Baltimore, John Beaver Mertie Jr. received a doctorate in geology from Johns Hopkins University. He was 23 and hungry for adventure. One spring day, armed with a letter of introduction from a professor, he went to see Alfred H. Brooks, head of the Alaska Division of the U.S. Geological Survey in Washington, D.C. As a student during the previous three summers, Mertie had worked as a USGS field assistant. A month later, he was on his way to Alaska.

The Territory of Alaska in 1911 was not a place for the faint or frail. To reach it, Mertie rode a cross-country train to Seattle, a steamship to Skagway, and the White Pass & Yukon Route Railroad through the mountains to Whitehorse, Yukon Territory. In Whitehorse, he boarded the first steamboat of the season to ply the Yukon River to Eagle, Alaska, bypassing Dawson City, which was under quarantine due to an outbreak of smallpox.

In the field, Mertie took to Alaska with gusto. A bearlike youth, he slogged through

John Beaver Mertie poses outside his home in Bethesda Md. in 1975. A bearlike man in his youth, Mertie spent 30 summers and a winter exploring Alaska. The Mertie Mountains near Eagle are named for him. (Jane Mangus)

swamps and fought mosquitos, worked with packhorses, forded and swam across streams. By fall, as he returned eastward, Alaska had hooked John Mertie for life. He returned for some 30 seasons of geologic field work, spanning nearly 60 years.

Mertie spent his first four field seasons in interior and southcentral Alaska mapping rocks and gold deposits near Eagle, copper-bearing rocks in the Copper River valley and coal in the Matanuska Valley. In 1915, he became a full-fledged geologist and began his first independent work, a study of placer gold deposits near Iditarod, in southwestern Alaska. When work was done that fall, the scientists auctioned their packhorses. Miners anted up $1,200 in gold — paper money was not yet in use in Alaska.

The 1917 field season began with a close call for Mertie in Lituya Bay, in the western part of what is now Glacier Bay National Park. Mertie was to map a nickel deposit that had been reported near the bay's head. He chartered a boat in Ketchikan with a capable captain and engineer.

Lituya Bay is a long body of water with a narrow entrance that is negotiable only at slack tide. At other times, swift tidal currents pour through a narrow opening guarded by reefs. In 1786, French explorer La Perouse watched two small boats come to grief on the rocks at a cost of 21 lives. Mertie and his companions nearly met a similar fate when the captain misjudged the tide by a quarter-hour and entered the bay's mouth too soon. On their second try, they safely sailed in. They found the rocks Mertie had been dispatched to map.

During the rest of the 1917 field season, Mertie toured gold mines on the Kenai

Peninsula and mapped a body of chromium ore east of Seldovia. He hitched a ride on a riverboat bound for gold-mining tributaries of the Susitna River. When the boat's anchor became mired in mud, he dove into cold Cook Inlet to dig it up. Later he perched atop a horse-drawn wagon as it rolled over rutted roads, not learning until he was underway that the jouncing wagon bore dynamite.

Visiting mines was always one of Mertie's favorite activities, and he counted many a prospector among his friends. Sam

John Beaver Mertie displays ptarmigan killed during the one winter he spent in Alaska in 1924. Mertie roamed much of the eastern part of Alaska doing geological work for the U.S. Geological Survey. (Courtesy of Marvin D. Mangus)

Peckovitch mined for gold on Admiralty Island, west of Juneau. Peckovitch had a penchant for straight-line paths through the mountains, seldom the safest or easiest route. One day as they chatted away, Mertie trailed Peckovitch down a steep mountainside, jumping down drops and winding up on a ledge from which there seemed to be no way down and no retreat. "I was standing there," Mertie later recalled, "pondering our dilemma when to my surprise and amazement Sam suddenly jumped out and grasped the uppermost branches of a spruce tree several feet away." Putting his weight on a branch, he bent it toward Mertie until he could grasp it. As they climbed down the tree and descended the mountain, Peckovitch talked on as if nothing had happened.

From 1921 to 1931, except for a 1924 winter-to-summer trek to Barrow, Mertie mapped the geology of the Yukon-Tanana region of the Interior. In fall 1921, to catch a steamship to Seattle, he joined a five-car caravan over the primitive road from Fairbanks to Valdez. The procession was led by the local marshal, who was escorting three men on their way to an insane asylum in Morningside, Ore., and two convicted murderers being sent to prison in Seattle. The trip took five muddy days. When an axle broke on his car, Mertie helped carve a replacement from a sapling. The next spring, he happily rode to Fairbanks on rails: Train service between Seward and Fairbanks started in 1922.

Mertie spent part of a single winter in Alaska, in 1924. The USGS wanted to investigate oil seeps reported east of Barrow, but the area was still beyond the reach of bush airplanes. In February, four scientists

John Beaver Mertie shows off a caribou rack just after breakup along the Killik River on the north slide of the Brooks Range. (Courtesy of Marvin D. Mangus)

and four assistants set off from Tanana, on the Yukon River, to cross the Brooks Range on dogsleds and set up a base camp on the frozen Killik River. From there, after the spring thaw, they planned to canoe to the Arctic Ocean. The trip went more or less as planned but was so arduous and took so long that there was little opportunity to study the oil seeps. Six years later, such expeditions were obsolete as airplanes began to range ever more broadly across the Alaskan Bush.

Mertie began to travel by plane during the 1930s. In 1935, he chartered a pair of float-equipped planes from Anchorage to

the Tikchik Lakes, fiordlike freshwater jewels in southwestern Alaska. The planes were so heavily laden they could not take off from Spenard Lake but had to launch from Cook Inlet. That fall, Mertie described his work to J.P. Hannon on Alaska's first radio broadcasting station, which Hannon himself had built.

In 1936, Mertie returned to Alaska's Interior, but his field season ran aground before it started. Bound out of Whitehorse on the riverboat *Klondike*, the steamer struck a reef and sank. Passengers and crew all made it ashore in a pair of leaking lifeboats. Two men went inland to tap a telegraph line and wire for help. The travelers were picked up within hours, but most of Mertie's equipment was lost in the mishap.

In 1939, Mertie took his wife, Mary, to Alaska, to give her a taste of the people and places he had so often spun stories about. They traveled to Fairbanks by steamship and rail, then Mertie flew to Nome to study tin deposits on the Seward Peninsula. Mary traveled to Circle with the mail carrier, rode a riverboat to Whitehorse and returned from there to Baltimore. That fall, awaiting a ship in Skagway, Mertie, 51, suffered an attack of heart fibrillation. "When it did not let up I was sure I was a goner," he later recalled, "so I quickly arose and signed all my vouchers and other field papers in order that my accounts could be cleared." By morning, he felt better. A heart rhythm problem persisted but so did Mertie, who lived another 41 years.

Three summers later, Mertie began to feel he was too old for the rigors of Alaskan field work. After 1942, he shifted his efforts to other geological problems, chiefly in the southeastern United States, and to mathematical matters which had always intrigued him. He retired at age 70, in 1958, but continued to work. Six years later, Mary Mertie died. John remarried in 1966. Evelyn, his second wife, had been an Atomic Energy

Some of John Beaver Mertie's field work in Alaska was done before the age of the airplane. In February 1924, he set off by dogsled from Tanana on the Yukon River, crossed through the Brooks Range and established a base camp on the Killik River. From here, he and his companions planned to travel by canoe to Barrow and explore the oil seeps reported to the east. (Courtesy of Marvin D. Mangus)

Commission scientist when they had met, 20 years earlier. She recorded his tales of Alaska and compiled them into a book, *Thirty Summers and A Winter* (1982), published after his death.

Mertie revisited Alaska three times late in his life to complete work begun in 1937 on the platinum deposits of Goodnews Bay, south of Kuskokwim Bay. Mertie's last Alaskan field work was in 1969, when he was 81 He published his last scientific paper in 1979 and died the following year, at age 92.

Mertie was a powerful man who left a rich and diverse legacy. He wrote more than 50 publications on Alaskan geology, including seminal works on the Yukon-Tanana Uplands, north and east of Fairbanks. His studies of mineral deposits in the Ruby-Iditarod region and the Goodnews Bay district are still cited today. For fun, he dabbled in theoretical mathematics. During the 1924 USGS expedition to Barrow, each man was allowed to bring only two books. Mertie brought a mathematics book and *The Faery Queene*, Elizabethan poet Edmund Spenser's heroic allegory of Protestant virtues.

After his death, a mountain range near Eagle was named in honor of John Beaver Mertie Jr. The Mertie Mountains span more than 100 miles between the Yukon and Tanana rivers, a tangible mark on the map of Alaska left by Mertie. But just as indelibly, Alaska left its mark on Mertie. He strode off the steamship in Skagway a young man in search of himself. On the mountains and glaciers, the ridge tops and rivers, in the wild animals and in the people he met, John Beaver Mertie found himself in Alaska.

Land Between the Mountains:
THE INTERIOR

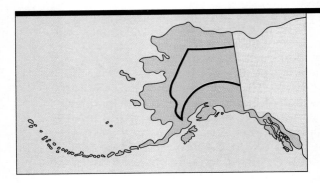

RIVERS, FURS AND GOLD WELD together the strands of the Interior's natural and cultural history. Taking in one-third of the state, the region reaches north from the crest of the Alaska Range to the crest of the Brooks Range, and west from the Canadian border to where the Athabaskan Indian culture gives way to that of the Eskimo. Although clusters of relatively low-lying mountains break the terrain, the Interior is primarily a huge river basin generally tilting from the Yukon-Tanana Uplands on the east to lowlands of the Bering Sea region on the west. The Yukon River, 2,300 miles long with 1,875 of those in Alaska, is the region's main artery, providing a corridor for movement of people and goods from early times to present.

As it flows across Alaska, the Yukon gathers in waters from several tributaries that themselves are among the longest rivers in the state. The Porcupine, Koyukuk, Tanana, Innoko and Birch Creek rank among Alaska's top 10 rivers in length. To the south in a separate valley that starts in the foothills of the Alaska Range, the Kuskokwim River begins its 700-mile journey to the Bering Sea.

The Yukon River supports one of the largest natural runs of king salmon in the world, with estimates of the number of fish reaching as high as half a million. When the salmon are running, fish wheels and nets are a common site along the banks of the Yukon and its tributaries.

The river valleys gain little elevation as they curve across Alaska; in some areas they meander across terrain so level that the areas are known as flats, bowls rimmed by uplands where river channels twist, turn, cross and recross, constantly rearranging channels, eating away old islands and creating new. Skeletons of half-buried riverboats and sinking cabins of sourdoughs testify to the rivers' capriciousness. Such areas give nightmares to navigators hoping to steer their craft through the maze. Yukon Flats, Minto Flats, Kaiyuh Flats — river captains know them well.

Waterfowl flock to the flats for these areas are some of the most productive habitat on the continent. Staff at the

A storm gathers over the East Fork Chandalar River valley in this view from Redsheep Creek, north of Arctic Village. (David G. Roseneau)

LEFT: *One of the best known views in the entire Brooks Range is that of the Arrigetch Peaks, 6,000-foot to 7,200-foot granite spires west of the Alatna River valley. Although the Brooks Range is not as high as the state's coastal mountains or Alaska Range, the seemingly endless mountain expanse from the Canadian border to the Chukchi Sea makes the Brooks Range one of the last and largest wilderness areas left in the United States. (Jon R. Nickles)*

ABOVE: *A juvenile common raven preens on top of a spruce tree in the Nenana River valley near Denali National Park. (David G. Roseneau)*

Yukon Flats refuge reported 30.9 ducks per square mile were produced on the refuge in 1991, with the primary species being lesser scaup, wigeon, green-winged teal, shovelers, pintails and mallards. Muskrats, beavers, river otters also find shelter here. And where there are fur-bearers, larger animals wait to prey on them. Bears, wolves, foxes roam the hills rimming the flats. Moose feed wherever the browse is good, and several herds of caribou range throughout the Interior. One bison herd grazes near the Farewell Burn area north of the Alaska Range and another near Delta. Dall sheep skip among rocky outcrops of the high mountains.

The Interior's climate, at least in winter, perhaps best matches the stereotype of Alaska's super cold winters. Record lows have been recorded here. At Prospect Creek, the temperature dipped to minus 80 in 1971. The area around Northway near the Canadian border frequently marks the state's coldest point. But just as the Interior is cold in the winter, it revels in warmth in the summer. Fort Yukon notched Alaska's highest recorded temperature of 100 degrees in 1915.

The sun shines almost 24 hours a day in summer but is fleeting in winter. Fairbanks has a summer maximum of 21 hours, 49 minutes of daylight, and a winter minumum of 3 hours, 42 minutes. The first frost typically arrives in September and much of the land stays frozen until early May.

A visit to the Interior in late summer or fall offers vistas of rolling hillsides shimmering with the golden leaves of birch, aspen and poplar, and speckled with the dark green of spruce needles. The state has designated some of the forest as the Tanana Valley State Forest. These forests, part of the circumpolar woodlands known as the taiga, provide fuel for wood stoves, the prime heat source for Bush dwellers scattered throughout the region.

According to some theories, the Interior, because of its position away from the sea coast, had ice-free pockets during the Ice Age. These pockets could have joined to form corridors allowing passage of ancient man to and through the region. Archaeologists maintain that man has lived in Alaska for at least 12,000 years, perhaps much

longer. The ancient people who evolved their culture in the Interior came to be called Athabaskan Indians. Their mobile lifestyle required small groups of hunters capable of moving quickly after game. For the most part, Athabaskans did not establish large permanent villages as did the Natives in Southeast and Southcentral.

Furs drew the first Westerners to the Interior. Hudson's Bay Co. explorers pushed over the mountains of northwestern Canada into the upper reaches of the Yukon drainage to expand the boundaries of their company's fur empire. In 1844, Scottish trader John Bell was the first white man known to have looked upon the Yukon River. Three years later, the company directed Alexander Murray to build a trading post, Fort Yukon, near the confluence of the Yukon and Porcupine rivers, to control fur trading on the upper river.

The Russians sent exploring and trading parties up the Yukon from their post at St. Michael on the Bering Sea coast. A buffer zone upriver from Tanana near Rampart Canyon separated the two trading empires.

As the mining frontier eclipsed that of the fur trade,

The Fortymile River — the South Fork is shown here — and portions of its tributaries have been designated a wild and scenic river. The stream winds through one of the Interior's first gold mining districts, where strikes in 1886 drew prospectors to the rolling, forested hills south of the Yukon River. Miners formed the community of Fortymile just over the Yukon boundary in Canada and spread out from there to strikes in the Klondike and near Circle City. Today, placer mining continues in the Fortymile District, and the Taylor Highway, which connects Eagle on the Yukon River with the Alaska Highway, runs through Fortymile country. (George Wuerthner)

FACING PAGE: *Fairbanks, population 30,843, lies along the banks of Chena Slough, an offshoot of the Tanana River. The city, Alaska's second largest, has been subject to flooding, but a water control project has alleviated this hazard in recent years.* (Steve McCutcheon)

RIGHT: *Third-generation Alaskan Cheryl Dick puts the finishing touches on a moosehide that is fleshed for tanning.* (Colleen Herning-Wickens)

enterprising prospectors, trappers and traders worked their way into the region, mostly by following the river valleys. From their efforts came the initial western settlements in the Interior, Circle City and Eagle. They served the trappers, the miners or both.

For decades, a series of gold strikes sent the population of the region scurrying from one site to another, paying scant attention to the international border with Yukon Territory when the prospect of riches was reported from the other side. Some of the settlements these prospectors founded became permanent; others faded with time. Fortymile in 1886, Circle City in 1893, Dawson City in 1896, Fairbanks in 1902, Innoko in 1906, Ruby in 1907, Iditarod in 1908 and Livengood in 1914, all brought people into the Interior. And people required transportation and other services.

Shallow-bottomed paddlewheelers took to the rivers, moving people and goods from one settlement to another. The military blazed a road from Eagle to Valdez, and strung telegraph lines to connect the region with Outside.

Geography and a bit of good fortune combined to spur establishment of a trading camp that grew into the region's largest community. E.T. Barnette had hired a riverboat captain to take him up the Tanana River to where the Valdez to Eagle military road crossed the river. Shallow water prevented the riverboat from advancing any farther than Chena Slough, where Barnette and his supplies were put ashore. A short time later, prospector

Felix Pedro struck gold while roaming the hills near the slough. Barnette saw an impending need for his supplies, and set up shop in 1901. The camp grew into a center of commerce and culture, named Fairbanks in 1902 after Theodore Roosevelt's vice president, Charles Fairbanks. Rails connected the town with the Gulf of Alaska in 1923. The university, founded as Alaska Agricultural College and School of Mines, was opened in 1922. The military noticed Fairbanks just prior to World War II, establishing Ladd Field, the first Army airfield in the state. And the Alaska Highway, another World War II project, was begun in 1942 to connect Fairbanks with the Lower 48. The sprawling city on the north side of the Tanana River valley grew to be the second largest in the state and the commercial center for much of northern Alaska.

In many respects, mining and trapping remain major economic forces in the Interior. Fairbanks' economy has diversified, adding jobs in government, the military, services and tourism. Some communities along the Alaska Highway and the George Parks Highway coming north from Anchorage earn income from tourism. But most of the region's other settlements depend on mining or subsistence or both.

The Usibelli Coal Mine, currently the state's only operating coal mine, fuels the economy of Healy on the Parks Highway. In 1991 Usibelli produced about 1.5 million short tons of coal worth about $45 million. About 50 percent of the coal went to power plants in the Interior to generate electricity; the Alaska Railroad carried the balance to Seward for shipment to South Korea.

About 20 miles northeast of Fairbanks, Amax Gold Inc. of Golden, Colo. is going ahead with plans to mine a large, low-grade gold-bismuth deposit, known as Fort Knox. Another area around Central, a few miles in from the Yukon River at Circle City, has been a center of placer

mining since pioneer days. Prospectors have been scouring the creeks and hills in the Fortymile District off the Taylor Highway between the Alaska Highway and Eagle for more than a century.

Birch Creek, Livengood, Hogatza, Ruby and Manley Hot Springs are other centers of placer mining. At Iditarod, pioneer families continue to prospect the creeks. One of the few Interior roads of any distance not connected to the state system runs from Ruby on the Yukon south to the mines around Poorman. But naming several current and past mining centers does little justice to the importance of mining in the Interior. Throughout the region's history, mining has been a vibrant force in its economy.

The Interior has ample terrain for wilderness recreation. Denali National Park and Preserve sees the bulk of its use on the north flank of the Alaska Range. A road wanders

LEFT: *The Delta area in the Tanana Valley about 100 miles southeast of Fairbanks has been the site of state efforts to promote agriculture. Farmers have concentrated on raising barley and other grains that tolerate the northern growing environment. Capricious weather and uncertain markets have discouraged some farmers, but the Delta area remains a supply and population center. From left, Mounts Hayes, Hess and Deborah dominate the Alaska Range skyline. (Steve McCutcheon)*

BOTTOM LEFT: *Another of the early mining communities is Circle City, commonly called Circle, on the south bank of the Yukon River at the terminus of the Steese Highway 125 miles northeast of Fairbanks. A strike at Birch Creek spurred Circle's growth into the largest mining town on the Yukon River before gold was found in the Klondike in 1896. Today, Circle is a terminus for boaters on the Yukon River, a supply point for trappers in Yukon flats and for miners working the hills inland from the river near Central. (Gil Mull)*

FACING PAGE: *The trans-Alaska oil pipeline crosses the South Fork of the Koyukuk River in its 800-mile journey from Prudhoe Bay to Valdez. The pipeline sometimes runs above ground, sometimes below, to counteract the effects of permafrost. (Steve McCutcheon)*

more than 90 miles through the park to the mining area of Kantishna.

White Mountain National Recreation Area and Steese National Conservation Areas encompass much of the region between Fairbanks and the Yukon River. Chena River State Recreation Area provides swimming and outdoor recreation for Fairbanks residents. Those who relish solitude and pristine waters head for Yukon-Charley River National Preserve. Several national wildlife refuges protect valuable habitat, and true backcountry adventurers seek the remoteness of Gates of the Arctic National Park or the Arctic National Wildlife Refuge whose borders overlap the Interior and Arctic regions. Beyond the Gates, where the mountains ease into a tundra-blanketed plain, lies Alaska's Arctic.

Denali

On February 16, 1917, the government officially recognized the crown jewel of Alaska's federal lands, Mount McKinley National Park, known since 1980 as Denali National Park and Preserve. The state's most visited attraction, Denali encompasses the towering mass of Mount McKinley (often called Denali by Alaskans, but still officially designated McKinley after the senator from Ohio who later became the country's 25th president), flanking segments of the Alaska Range and foothills, and the forested and tundra-covered lowlands on the north side drifting away toward Lake Minchumina.

Most visitors to Denali ride buses or sign on for tours along the park's only road, a 90-mile, gravel route skirting the northern foothills. During the summer, private cars are prohibited beyond mile 14 without a special permit. Hikers may get on and off the buses at will, except in a few areas particularly sensitive to wildlife. Designated campgrounds are strung out along the Park Road, and abundant lodging and meal services welcome visitors just outside the park entrance.

For some years government officials and private businesses have discussed opening additional visitor facilities on the south side of the Alaska Range to ease some of the pressure on the current visitor hub. Various schemes have suggested using land near Denali State Park, or out the Petersville Road, both in Southcentral, for this new development. In spring 1992, efforts were focused on opening a visitor center at Talkeetna, headquarters for many of the air taxis that offer flightseeing to Mount McKinley and jumping off point for most of the climbers who seek to scale North America's highest peak. No decisions have yet been finalized, and the search for a second visitor hub for Alaska's number one visitor attraction continues.

Rafting the Nenana River is one of the favorite activities for visitors to Denali. The river swings through Cantwell and heads north through the Alaska Range on the eastern border of the park. Rafters usually put in south of the Riley Creek entrance area, and float north through Nenana Canyon to an area near Healy. (Dean Abramson)

TOP LEFT: *This red fox has had a successful hunt, bringing back an arctic ground squirrel and a willow ptarmigan. Red foxes can be found throughout Denali country in appropriate habitat. (John W. Warden)*

LEFT: *Visitors to Denali can watch for Dall sheep, the only wild white sheep, on cliffs above Nenana Canyon near the park entrance, and at several rocky overlooks along the Park Road. Campers staying at Igloo Campground have good access to the Dall sheep*

herd grazing on rocky outcrops just to the west. (Charles Kay)

ABOVE: *Moose are common in forested areas of Denali. These largest members of North America's deer family breed in late September and early October, with females in good health and with good range giving birth to twins from 15 percent to 60 percent of the time. Males lose their antlers in winter, and grow new ones in May. (Charles Kay)*

Far North Living

By Stuart Pechek

Editor's note: *Photographer, writer, trapper and seasonal biological worker Stuart Pechek usually makes his home in Fairbanks, when he is not out in the Bush.*

It may not be complete happiness, but sitting by a comforting fire in one of the most remote cabins in the northern Interior comes close. Especially when it is 50 degrees below. On the south slopes of the Brooks Range where I work a winter trapline, the world's cold fitfully makes itself at home, a testimony to my all-too-often frostbitten nose and cheeks.

Coming to Alaska 18 years back, I often dreamed of the bush wilderness. In 1978, the mystique of the Brooks Range lured me into a four-month sojourn. Starting at Kaktovik, an Eskimo village on the arctic coastal plain near Canada, I wandered south into the mountains and then westward several hundred miles to Anaktuvuk Pass, an inland Eskimo settlement. That led to a chance meeting with a trapper in Arctic Village who told me of an unused cabin in the eastern Brooks Range. That changed my life.

Instead of migrating to warmer climes and snuffing out the Fairbanks winter blues, I began to fly north by ski plane, seeking a life of simplicity and solitude, centered around this log cabin in the Arctic National Wildlife Refuge.

It is within this 10-foot by 13-foot home that basic survival becomes a priority and enjoyment. I appreciate the warmth from every spruce stick tossed into the stove, cut and hauled from the arctic forest.

Without a nearby store, food becomes an obsession. A simple pilot bread (cracker) and jam turns into a culinary delight. I fly in the basic staples like flour, eggs, and of course, chocolate goodies. If I am lucky, I shoot a caribou nearby for meat. In other winters

LEFT: *Stuart Pechek readies for a check of his trapline on the south slope of the Brooks Range. He stays in wall tents when he is out on the trapline. (Marta McWhorter)*

FACING PAGE: *A full moon hangs over this December scene at the northern fringes of the taiga in the Sheenjek River valley. Stuart Pechek's cabin and cache are 50 miles from the nearest neighbor and 200 miles from the nearest road. (Stuart Pechek)*

these restless creatures cannot be found.

The essential element in my winter diet is fats — lots of butter and bacon — something most people avoid and I crave. I can eat as much as I desire and still lose weight, the art of cold weather dieting. Long days in the arctic cold zap energy and greatly increase metabolism. On a low-fat diet of past years I have struggled to stay warm.

Four winters ago a marten broke into the cache, stealing all my butter. I panicked, crawling through the brush for a day until I recovered one pound of that caloric gold.

The cabin rests on a lake but water is not easily obtained. By midwinter, the ice depth sinks past 6 feet and the shallows extend out much too far. Wind-packed snow chunks are trundled to the cabin and melted in an empty five-gallon Blazo can.

There are many beautiful places in Alaska,

and some, rightfully astounding. To me, none can match the pure and simple beauty of the arctic boreal forest in winter. Much of that enchantment is steeped in a ubiquitous stillness blanketing the country. When viewed from a hillside above the cabin and after fresh snow, the spruce appear like a surreal patchwork of cardboard cutouts poked into a cavern floor and projecting like black stalagmites dipped in cream.

Just north of the cabin these evergreens give way to spacious tundra, wavering and

LEFT: *Trapper Pechek boards and stretches a marten skin. (Marta McWhorter)*

BOTTOM LEFT: *Stuart Pechek tends to kitchen chores in his 10-foot by 13-foot cabin in the Brooks Range. (Marta McWhorter)*

thinning themselves on the march northward through growing mountains until only few remain — trees no more than 3 inches thick yet a few centuries old.

But it is the light — or lack of it — that casts mysterious moods to the land. In winter's black heart the night squashes the sun below the southern horizon for six weeks and allows a mere three hours of daylight daily before clamping the lid again. During this period I scuttle quickly over the trails with snowshoes, eking out every second of available light.

In December the full moon also pushes forth, banding the northern sky in alpenglow and a crimson-purple haze. Spellbound on the trails I can only believe that the earth has somehow left me.

Perhaps the true soul of this broad land lies in its freedom from man's meddlings. The closest road, which leads to Fairbanks along the trans-Alaska pipeline, is more than 200 miles away; my nearest neighbor, one quarter of that. If I were to step out my cabin door, I could probably walk through the Brooks Range, onto the North Slope, and over the arctic ice pack until I reached the North Pole — without seeing any marks of mankind.

My winter existence centers around snowshoeing a 70-mile network of fingered trails, threading through frozen creeks, forests and tundra. I predominantly trap pine marten, with a goal of leaving a strong population for years.

Seven-foot snowshoes propel me over the fluffy snow, at times the density of soap suds, keeping my heavy body somewhat aloft. In years past, before using the seven-footers, yearly trailbreaking was sometimes like a death march with me sinking to my thighs with every step.

While checking the lines, Melozi, that ever-so-faithful husky, drags a sled laden with trapping supplies, my gear and enough food for a week. At nights I am ensconced in tiny wall tents outfitted with wood stoves. The warmth and luxury of drying out gear becomes priceless.

Dressing for the cold dictates wise decisions and I religiously follow the layering system, eyeballing the temperature closely. All the how-to books state that sweating is a no-no; that is much easier said than done.

After years of experimentation, I can usually wrap myself adequately in light layers of polypropylene and wool garments down to 30 below. From there to oblivion, I wear heavyweights: a down parka, thicker underwear, fuzzy mitts and a beaver hat worn over a fat balaclava.

Generally, most trappers harbor close to home when the temperature slides below minus 40. However, two winters ago the temperature hibernated in the minus 50s and 60s for five consecutive weeks. After several days of staying inside, cabin fever began to build, a psychological desire to escape the confines or scream forever. Shortly, I ventured forth over the lines and continued to travel throughout the cold snap.

In the deep cold prevention is everything.

By myself most of the time, accidents like breaking a leg would be fatal. If I fell through river ice (a fear I always carry) and could extricate myself, my life would be measured in the seconds it took to start a fire. I always carry a waterproof container of matches in a pant's pocket. Luckily this country provides ample spruce with dead and tinder-dry lower branches.

Furthermore, the extremely dense and calm air from the crazy cold creates a giant amphitheater. A finger snap at 100 feet sounds like an arm's length away. Trees pop and groan from the heavy air and can be heard from far beyond.

During one frozen day, I was startled every time by the slight whisk of brush flicking off my snowshoes. It sounded like someone dragging sticks along a picket fence.

No matter what the temperature, seeing winter wildlife on the trail always cheers me, even though sightings are few — another component of the North's mystique. For some reason Monument Creek has seemed most hospitable.

As I rounded a hairpin bend one day, several timber wolves dashed past me into thick willows. However, one cream-colored fellow in puffed-out fur plopped down on his haunches. For several minutes we gazed in mutual curiosity until he arose and strolled into the bushes.

Shortly after I listened to the pack yowling around me, their choruses echoing from the valley walls.

As I snowshoed along the creek bed another day, a great gray owl suddenly burst from the spruce forest, dark with depth. It descended like a giant apparition silhouetted against the cobalt sky, then seemingly vaporized into the opposite bank's trees. Had I momentarily been looking elsewhere, I would have missed it.

Nonetheless, trying to understand the never-ending saga of predator-prey relationships is truly observed in the wild animal tracks. This mountainous region contains a healthy diversity of furbearers and wildlife, some seasonal.

Marten, wolverine, weasel, red fox, wolf, moose, caribou and snowshoe hare are sometimes abundant. The country also supports to a lesser degree: lynx, mink, river otter, beaver, muskrat and arctic fox, an occasional visitor that wanders over the mountains from the North Slope.

Through tracks and some imagination I have watched wolves bound through deep snow in pursuit of moose. Other tracks show where a lynx waits patiently for prey. Tucked into willows along a frozen lake's edge, this wild cat watches a red fox hunting along the shoreline for voles. At long last the unaware fox wanders within 20 feet of the lynx, crouched in tense energy. Suddenly the lynx explodes from cover. The fox reacts but is caught within several strides. This story was etched in razor-clear tracks, which led to a half-eaten fox carcass in the bushes. There is so much to learn about the relationship of wildlife to the land and to man. Every winter provides new chapters. I can only hope that I can continue to add to the knowledge and be part of this country. For this is a land I would trade for none.

Stuart Pechek and his dog, Melozi, cross Lynx Lake on their return from checking a trapline. Pechek traps mostly pine marten, but notes the signs of several other wildlife species on his winter jaunts. (Marta McWhorter)

Alaska's Far North:
THE ARCTIC

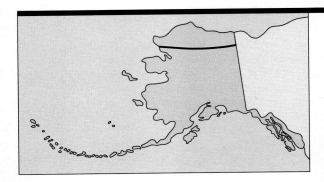

NORTH OF THE BROOKS RANGE, Alaska sweeps in a broad, tundra-covered, river-laced plain to the Arctic Ocean. This is the Arctic, the frozen North of myth. In northwestern Alaska, the region adopts the boundary between the North Slope Borough and the Northwest Arctic Borough, generally following the DeLong Mountains to the Chukchi Sea coast just south of Cape Thompson.

The DeLongs are one in a series of mountain groups, collectively known as the Brooks Range, that curve across northern Alaska into Canada. Tree growth reaches its northernmost limit here, with the south side of the Brooks Range heavily forested, while only a few, severely stunted spruce survive in sheltered niches beyond the mountains. Permafrost underlies most of the Arctic, prohibiting drainage and creating a soggy mat of tundra that stretches for hundreds of miles. On the hillsides, drying winds and freezing temperatures weather the rock into jagged gravel. It is sometimes difficult for hikers to decide which is more troublesome, slipping on loose gravel or tumbling headfirst off basketball-sized hummocks.

Cold temperatures, low precipitation and strong winds typify the Arctic's climate. The Arctic Ocean and Chukchi Sea moderate coastal temperatures somewhat. Even so, Barrow's summer high averages only 39 degrees; February, the coldest month, averages minus 19 degrees. Temperatures fluctuate more widely inland toward the Brooks Range where highs can reach the 70s or 80s and lows drop to 30s and 40s below, and sometimes colder. Umiat, on the Colville River just north of the Brooks Range, frequently records the state's coldest temperatures.

Because it lies north of the Arctic Circle, the sun does not set over the Arctic for part of the summer and does not rise for two months in winter. At Barrow, the sun remains below the horizon from November 18 to January 24.

An extremely short growing season compels plants to bloom and form seeds as efficiently as possible. Many plants do adapt to these conditions, bursting forth in a

Caribou in a herd numbering about 60,000 move past the Turner River in the extreme northeastern corner of the Arctic. Alaska's two largest caribou herds and a couple of smaller ones spend the summer on the North Slope, calving and feeding before beginning their fall journey south through the Brooks Range. (Jo Overholt)

giant mosaic of color each June. Arnica, lupine, glacier avens, cushion hawk's beard and cottongrass mix with willow and alder shrubs along the river valleys.

Readers might conclude that such a harsh climate would limit wildlife in the region, but the Arctic in summer has some of the greatest concentrations of wildlife on the continent. Grizzly bears, wolves, red and arctic foxes, musk ox, arctic ground squirrels, lemmings, voles and a host of bird life breed and feed on the region's tundra. Two great caribou herds — Western Arctic and Porcupine — and a couple of smaller ones migrate each summer to the Arctic to calve. The Porcupine herd, 180,000 animals strong, travels through the Brooks Range

Folded brown sandstones and conglomerates and gray limestones are visible in this view looking south into the heart of the northeastern Brooks Range. (Arne Bakke)

from the Interior and from Canada's central Yukon Territory; the 415,000-member Western Arctic herd treks from wintering grounds in the Selawik Lowlands through the mountains to the lowlands inland from Point Lay for the summer. Moose, normally a species that prefers forests, have worked their way through the mountains to foothills along the upper Colville River. Shore areas and offshore ice are the home of the polar bear, walrus and a variety of seals, and bowhead whales feed each summer in the Beaufort Sea.

The Arctic is also home of the Inupiat Eskimo, who live in eight communities spread out from Point Hope on the Chukchi coast to Kaktovik near Canada and inland to Anaktuvuk Pass, last home of the Nunamiut or Inland Eskimo. Until oil development came to the region in 1968, almost all of the Arctic's residents lived by subsistence,

TOP LEFT: *A male king eider rests on a mat of tundra on the arctic coastal plain. In Alaska, this species breeds along almost the entire arctic coast from Point Hope to Demarcation Point, at the Canadian border. (John W. Warden)*

ABOVE: *With curiosity and a bit of trepidation, these arctic fox kits keep close watch on a photographer. Arctic foxes — these two are in their summer coat — occur naturally across the northern and western coasts of Alaska to as far south as the northwestern shore of Bristol Bay. (Gary Schultz)*

FACING PAGE: *The Dalton Highway approaches the Brooks Range on its run from Prudhoe Bay to the Interior's Elliott Highway. Formerly called the North Slope Haul Road, the route was built to support construction of the trans-Alaska pipeline and is named for Jim Dalton, arctic engineer involved in early oil development. (Steve McCutcheon)*

RIGHT: *High up on the list of Alaska's predators is the wolf. Wolves prey on caribou, especially as they approach the foothills and mountains on the migrations, moose and smaller mammals. Their calls to other members of the wolf pack are among the Arctic's most vivid images. (Roy M. Corral)*

supplemented in a few cases by government employment. Coastal Eskimos hunted marine mammals, ptarmigan, foxes and caribou. They picked greens in the short summers, preserving some of them in seal oil. The Inland Eskimos in particular relied on caribou, trading with coastal residents for products of the sea.

Following the explorers, many of whom came in search of Sir John Franklin and his lost expedition or sought the Northwest Passage, the first white men to linger in the Arctic served as traders and government agents. Others were New England whaling men. Charles Brower, James Allen and a few others remained for decades, forming dynasties that continue today.

By far the most dramatic change to hit the region, frequently called the North Slope or simply the slope, was the discovery of oil near Prudhoe Bay in 1968. The find led to development of a major industrial complex on the coastal plain; construction of the Haul Road, now designated the Dalton Highway, from Prudhoe to Livengood on the Elliott Highway in the Interior; and parallel construction of the trans-Alaska pipeline to carry the oil 800 miles south to Valdez. Industrial development, feeder pipelines and roads have spread across the coastal plain as other oil deposits have been drilled.

Modernization has come to the communities also. The North Slope Borough earns big tax dollars from the oil, and in the 1970s launched a construction program of modern school buildings complete with swimming pools, office buildings, houses. Where once hunters used snares, skin boats and handcrafted harpoons, they now use snowmachines, high-powered rifles and harpoons carrying explosives.

The search for oil continues in the Arctic, with efforts focused on the region east of Prudhoe Bay. Geologists look beyond the Canning River to the coastal plain of the Arctic National Wildlife Refuge. Those who support the integrity of refuges and others who believe in the value of

FACING PAGE: *This view looks up the Hulahula River valley toward the Brooks Range. The Hulahula begins at a glacier, winds through the Romanzof Mountains, squirts through a canyon and enters the coastal plain for a 50-mile run to Camden Bay just west of Kaktovik. (Bill Sherwonit)*

ABOVE: *Robert Aikens and his whale crew paddle just off his shore-ice camp near Barrow. This photo, taken several years ago, shows the traditional skin boat formerly used by Eskimo hunters. Whalers today frequently use motorized aluminum skiffs. (Staff)*

LEFT: *Kaktovik residents gather on the shore to watch the butchering of a bowhead whale on Barter Island. Bowheads, among the largest of baleen whales, swim north each spring from the southern Bering Sea, through Bering Strait, along the Chukchi coast and east along the arctic coast to the Beaufort Sea, their summer feeding grounds. The Eskimo Whaling Commisson and federal government representatives meet to set quotas for the taking of bowheads. Each season each whaling village from St. Lawrence Island north and east to Kaktovik is allotted a number of kills and strikes (where a whale is struck but not recovered). If one village does not use its quota, it can give its unused portion to another village farther along the whales' migratory path. (Kathy O'Reilly-Doyle)*

BOTTOM LEFT: *Jenny Paniak Wells, with Stacy on her back, digs marrow from a caribou leg bone at her home in Anaktuvuk Pass. On the cutting board are slices of muktuk, and Simon helps himself to a small pile of fish. (Penny Rennick)*

FACING PAGE: *Forget-me-nots and other wild flowers brighten the cliffs where seabirds, including 50,000 murres, nest at Cape Thompson. The spit on which the community of Point Hope is located is in the background. (David G. Roseneau)*

wilderness return their gaze. The refuge's coastal plain is narrower than that of the Arctic farther west because here the mountains push closer to the sea. This plain is the traditional center of calving for the Porcupine caribou herd. On a barrier island offshore sits Kaktovik. Whether there is oil underneath the refuge's coastal plain is unknown. What is on the coastal plain are musk ox feeding, butting heads and cavorting across the tundra; foxes raising their kits in tunneled mounds; Lapland longspurs with their chicks nestled in cups of grass; foraging golden plovers and buff-breasted sandpipers, and hunting snowy and short-eared owls. Refuge staff have counted more than a hundred species of birds, 40 of fish and about that many of mammals on refuge lands. Some humans count wilderness among the refuge's values; others count oil. The controversy continues.

Marvin Peter's Inupiat Family Album

By Christoper Wooley, Karen Brewster, Jana Harcharek, Dorothy Edwardsen and Mabel Panigeo

Editor's note: *The authors are present or former staff of the North Slope Borough Inupiat History, Language and Culture Commission (IHLC).*

Marvin Sagvan Peter (1911-1962) created baleen baskets and produced hundreds of photographs admired by people on Alaska's North Slope and beyond. Marvin was the son of reindeer herder Peter Takkak and Betsy Qaaqattak of Nuvuk (Point Barrow). He and his sisters Ida Numnik and Olive Kanayurak, and his brother John Peter, were members of one of the last families to live at Nuvuk. They were born into an Inupiat community that was adapting to the global political and economic changes of the 20th century. Marvin's life was linked to the land through hunting and the use of natural materials in his crafts, and he became associated with Outsiders through the sale of his crafts.

Marvin was a talented baleen basket-maker and is remembered as always having a camera around his neck. He made money by selling his baskets to trading ships, and would then buy groceries for the family. He later worked as a janitor and taught basketry and crafts at the Barrow school, and his students sold the baskets through a co-op in Juneau. "We liked going to his class. …We could speak Eskimo in Marvin's class," according to Harry Brower, Sr. of Barrow. Native children in those days were normally forbidden to speak their own language in school. Harry recalls Marvin telling them traditions about Nuvuk that Marvin learned as a boy from his father. Pauline Burkher, who taught at the Barrow school between 1937 and 1943, remembers Marvin as a good teacher who invented a basket-weave which the students could easily manage. His grandnephew, Danny Matumeak, recalls, "Marvin taught me to look at things differently. I am proud to have learned from him." Danny said Marvin taught him that quickly made baskets may sell, but "…patience brings in bigger money."

Marvin survived the flu epidemics that hit the Arctic during the early 1900s, and that brought Dr. Henry Greist and his wife Mollie, a nurse, to Barrow. When he was young though, Marvin was ill, possibly with

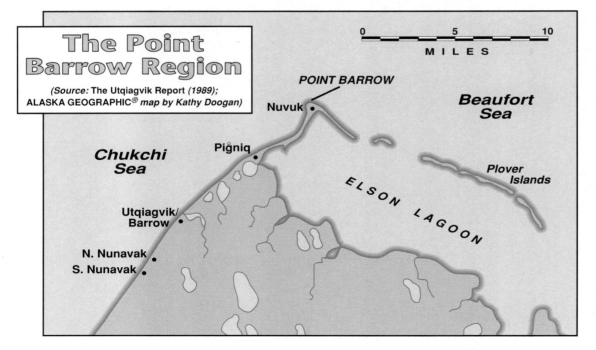

The Point Barrow Region

(*Source:* The Utqiagvik Report *(1989);*
ALASKA GEOGRAPHIC® *map by Kathy Doogan*)

POINT BARROW

Beaufort Sea

Chukchi Sea

Nuvuk

Piġniq

Plover Islands

ELSON LAGOON

Utqiagvik/ Barrow

N. Nunavak

S. Nunavak

0   5   10
MILES

polio. The illness put him in the Barrow Presbyterian Hospital under the Greists' care, and left him with a limp. He was a bachelor all his life, and he used to stay with the Greists occasionally. Mollie Greist collected bird specimens for Outside museums, and Marvin helped by skinning birds and blowing eggs. Dr. Greist was an avid photographer, and Marvin may have learned from him. His sister Ida told us that photography is in their family's blood, and she recalled that Marvin's uncle, Martin Sakiq, who died when Marvin was young, also had a camera. Marvin apparently was introduced to photography at a young age.

Marvin walked with a cane while in town and used crutches when walking out on the beach or tundra. He could not participate in whaling because of his crippled leg, but he helped with walrus and caribou hunting to

LEFT: *Marvin Peter (third from left) poses with other young Eskimos. With him are (from left) Lloyd Ahvakana, Martina Taalak, Eben Hopson and an unidentified young woman.*

ABOVE: *Walrus supplied food, skins and ivory for Barrow's residents. Even though a childhood illness left him with a limp, Marvin Peter helped with walrus hunting.*

obtain a share of the meat, and hunted ducks near Point Barrow, assisted by his younger brother, John Peter. Marvin lived by himself, but always shared food with his sisters and other members of his extended family. According to his sister Ida, "He was always working on something."

During a lull in the 1990 Alaska Eskimo Whaling Commission meeting in Barrow, Ida invited us to visit her at home and look

LEFT: *Julia Segevan and Ruth Talaak, wearing summer dress of parkas with a fur-lined ruff on the hood, stand on the deck of one of the ships that called at Barrow during the few weeks of open water in the Arctic Ocean.*

ABOVE: *Marvin Peter captured this elderly couple, Ilavgagruaq and Kivvauraq, outside a sod building.*

through her old photographs. We were chatting and leafing through a book about baleen basketry, which prompted Ida to mention that she had lots of Marvin's old pictures, and would we like to see them? Like so many old photos of relatives, the pictures were bent and worn, but they were numerous, varied and unique.

An old box of more than 400 negatives was with the photos, and several were negatives of the prints Ida had shown us. Some were in individual envelopes that were dated and labeled. Many were nitrate

negatives that were deteriorating and were a safety concern because of their flammability. Ida graciously donated the negatives to the North Slope Borough for conservation and restoration. Following the advice of Susan Kaplan, director of the Peary-MacMillan Arctic Museum in Brunswick, Maine, IHLC arranged for historic photo restorer David Mishkin to

produce duplicate safety negatives and prints. IHLC staff have analyzed many of the prints and recorded more information about people and events Marvin preserved on film. Fortunately, most images from prints of the unlabeled negatives can be identified by current North Slope elders.

An elder recently remarked that she recalled when Marvin took one of the photos — a treasured four-generation portrait of her family. Most of the photos date from the 1930s to 1950s, and many are portraits of grandparents of current North Slope Inupiat, as well as photos of couples, children, church and civic groups. There are also scenes of reindeer herding, sea mammal butchering, community events, ships, planes, animals and a photo of the first

June 1917

tourists to Barrow's Top of the World Hotel. Marvin preserved his ties to the community and to the land through his camera, and captured elusive emotions from Barrow's recent past. Marvin Peter's photo collection is an Inupiat family album and a visual record of his intimate connection to the land and its people.

Eskimo photographer Marvin Peter took this photo of (from left) Steven Segevan, Timothy Toovak and Alfred Koonaloak. Marvin Peter was born at Nuvuk (Point Barrow) and grew up in the Barrow area.

Out West:
THE BERING SEA COAST

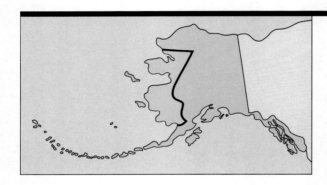

THE BERING SEA COAST REGION takes in much of western Alaska, excluding the Alaska Peninsula and the far northwestern corner. Its topography consists essentially of five river basins, the Seward Peninsula and a smaller upland where extensions of the Kuskokwim Mountains reach the sea between Bristol Bay and Kuskokwim Bay. The region stretches about 700 miles from Cape Seppings on the north to the north shore of Kvichak Bay on the south. Its eastern boundary follows the frontier between the Inupiat and Yup'ik Eskimo cultures of the coast and the Interior Athabaskan Indian culture.

Weather in the region acts a bit like a chameleon, changing dramatically, especially in spring and fall. Geography plays the biggest role in this change because during late spring and summer open water in the Bering Sea moderates temperatures. At these times, the region has a coastal climate. But for much of the year, all of the Chukchi Sea and much of the Bering is frozen over. Then the Bering acts more like an inland plain than a sea, and the region's weather patterns more closely resemble those of the Interior with extreme temperatures. In Nome, January temperatures average 6 degrees; July averages 50 degrees.

Of the five great rivers that enter saltwater in the region, two have combined to form the largest delta in Alaska, and one of the largest in the hemisphere. The Yukon and Kuskokwim rivers drain much of the state's interior, spreading their sediment seaward from Norton Sound to Kuskokwim Bay. The Noatak and Kobuk rivers dump their waters into Kotzebue Sound, and far to the south the Nushagak River drains a basin between the Kuskokwim Mountains and the Alaska Range. The main exception to the riverine topography is the Seward Peninsula, made up of a cluster of small mountain groups on the south and broad lowlands on the north.

Waterfowl and furbearers that favor watery habitat abound in this region of immense marshlands. The biggest wetland is the Yukon-Kuskokwim delta, much of which

Salmon hang to dry at the coastal settlement of Shishmaref, population 456, on the northwest shore of the Seward Peninsula. (Jon R. Nickles)

LEFT: *Walrus Islands State Game Sanctuary in Bristol Bay has one of the state's largest hauling-out grounds for walrus. The island can be reached by boat from Togiak, and visitors need a permit to go ashore. (Charlie Crangle)*

ABOVE: *One of five loon species found in Alaska, red-throated loons breed in suitable habitat throughout western Alaska. (USFWS)*

lies within Yukon Delta National Wildlife Refuge. At different times of the year, flocks of birds numbering in the millions use the refuge — some of the most important bird habitat in the Western Hemisphere. Geese, ducks, swans, shorebirds, raptors and perching birds either nest on or migrate through the area.

In the past decade, biologists have studied intensively four geese species — emperor, white-fronted, cackling Canada and brant — whose populations registered severe declines. 1991 surveys showed breeding populations up, but total populations slightly down for cacklers, white-fronts and emperors. The lower totals could reflect a true decline, but could be accounted for also by sampling error or by some environmental condition that was peculiar to 1991. For instance, that year was the first time in a great while that breeding grounds were free of snow and ice when the birds arrived. Thus more nesting habitat was available immediately over a wider area, a circumstance that may have affected the aerial counts.

The Yukon delta has the largest breeding concentrations of brant in the world. The small, dark geese require different techniques for counting, and most population estimates come from tallies on wintering grounds in Mexico. Brant numbers were down the last two years, with 93,200 recorded for 1991.

Anecia Lomack (left) and Anecia Toyukak pose with their kindergarten class at Manokotak, a community of 404 west of Dillingham within Togiak National Wildlife Refuge. (James A. Pickard)

LEFT: *Yup'ik Eskimos ice fish on the lower Yukon River near Russian Mission. People of the Russian Mission area refer to this type of fishing as hooking, and from mid-February to April their chief catch is burbot (lush) or northern pike. The burbot are usually boiled, occasionally baked; pike are commonly split, gutted and dried. (Harry M. Walker)*

BOTTOM LEFT: *Commercial salmon fishing contributes substantially to western Alaska's economy. One product of that fishery is salmon roe. In years past, salmon were stripped of their roe by hand. Mechanization has taken over in the 1990s. A butchering machine slits the belly and extracts the guts and eggs. They are sent to a sorting room where the eggs are graded by species. They are then put into an agitator to be cooked in a 100 percent brine solution with a secret ingredient to flavor the eggs. The agitator cooks the eggs anywhere from 19 to 23 minutes, depending in part on the size and freshness of the eggs. The eggs are then graded by color, packed in resealable plastic buckets and shipped to Japan. (Steve McCutcheon)*

FACING PAGE: *Gambell, population 525, is built on a gravel spit near the northwest tip of St. Lawrence Island. Formerly several villages were located on the island, but in the past several decades islanders have resettled into just two villages, Gambell and Savoonga. (Harry M. Walker)*

Snow geese from breeding colonies on Russia's Wrangel Island also use the delta on their migrations to and from the Pacific Northwest. The Tavener's Canada goose, a larger relative of the cackler, has a wider distribution and nests throughout the delta where its population seems to be increasing.

Biologists are also concerned about two duck species, spectacled and Steller's eiders. In 1991, spectacled eiders were nominated for threatened status under the Endangered Species Act. The bulk of this species breeds on the delta where less than 2,500 breeding pairs were counted in 1991. Steller's eider, which normally breed on the North Slope or Chukchi coast, have bred historically

ABOVE: *Headquarters for NANA Regional Corporation and the largest trading center in northwestern Alaska, Kotzebue is built on a spit jutting into Kotzebue Sound. Lt. Otto von Kotzebue (1787 - 1846) of the Imperial Russian Navy named the sound for himself during a cruise along the northwest Alaska coast in 1816 in search of the Northwest Passage. (Kathy O'Reilly-Doyle)*

RIGHT: *Nome, population 4,559, on the south shore of the Seward Peninsula, fronts Norton Sound. The town was born at the turn of the century when gold was found along the Nome River, in the beach gravels and in the benchlands back from the water. It has grown into the supply center for most of the Seward Peninsula and Norton Sound communities. (Penny Rennick)*

on the delta, but no longer do so. Rafts of non-breeding Steller's congregate each summer off Nunivak Island, but overall numbers of this species are down significantly enough to warrant its possible nomination to the threatened list.

The Yukon-Kuskokwim delta was once thought to be primarily geese breeding habitat, but recent censuses indicate that duck densities and total populations here are the highest in the state. Total duck breeding density is 8.5 broods per square mile; Yukon Flats in the Interior ranks next highest with 5.7 per square mile. In 1991, the Yukon-Kuskokwim delta produced 800,000 ducklings or 48 percent of the statewide total.

Three-quarters or more of the state's tundra swan population breeds on the delta, and the same percentage applies to shorebirds that number in the millions at different times of the year. Certain localized areas also support the state's highest breeding concentrations of some raptor species such as golden eagles, rough-legged hawks and gyrfalcons.

The delta itself harbors a collection of furbearers and

small mammals, many of which are actively trapped and hunted. Muskrats, mink, river otters, weasels and beavers are joined by hares, lynx and wolverines, and arctic and red foxes in the uplands. Musk ox roam Nunivak and Nelson islands and some adjacent mainland. A caribou herd is expanding in the Kilbuck Mountains to the southeast of Bethel and so are the wolves. Moose are increasing in river valleys surrounding the delta, although when they wander onto the flats they are quickly shot. Brown bears in the uplands are holding their own.

South of the delta and beyond the platinum mining country around Goodnews Bay lies Bristol Bay and Togiak National Wildlife Refuge. Rocky pinnacles at Cape Newenham harbor the state's largest mainland seabird colony, home to parakeet auklets, pigeon guillemots, pelagic and double-crested cormorants, common murres, black-legged kittiwakes, horned and tufted puffins and other species. The cape is also the northernmost large haulout for threatened Stellers sea lions, which congregate at Chagvan Bay each spring when the herring are running. East of the cape, Nanvak Bay is one of the largest haulouts and pupping areas for harbor seals. At neighboring Cape Peirce the largest mainland walrus colony in North America comes ashore.

In 1988, 146 caribou were reintroduced to Nushagak Peninsula, where they had not been seen for more than a century. The herd, made up mostly of females from the Alaska Peninsula herd near Becharof Lake, has thrived and in 1991 numbered more than 500, making it the fastest growing caribou herd in Alaska.

The caribou, marine mammals and seabirds, however, take a back seat to fish, for this is Bristol Bay where fish are

A kayaker pitches camp on a sand bar along the Noatak River, most of which runs through Noatak National Preserve in northwestern Alaska. The river flows about 425 miles, beginning in the central Brooks Range and ending in Kotzebue Sound, draining one of the largest river basins in the state. (Charlie Crangle)

FACING PAGE: *St. Matthew and Hall islands are two of the most remote spots in Alaska. This view of St. Matthew shows Bull Seal Point and Bull Seal Cove, and a joint U.S. Fish and Wildlife Service-National Oceanic and Atmospheric Administration field camp used by biologists studying seabirds. (David G. Roseneau)*

RIGHT: *Richard Randall, 5 when this photo was taken in 1986, shows off his pups at the Kobuk River village of Ambler. (Ron Miller)*

king. Commercial and sport fishing fuels the region's economy. Five species of salmon, rainbow trout, Dolly Varden, Arctic char, lake trout, grayling, northern pike and burbot entice anglers worldwide who make sport fishing the largest visitor activity in the region. The world's largest runs of sockeye salmon dominate a commercial salmon commerce valued at $108.7 million in 1991.

The Seward Peninsula reaches 200 miles from Alaska toward Asia north of the Yukon delta. Its farthest tip, Cape Prince of Wales, is the westernmost point in continental North America. Mining and reindeer herding bolster a subsistence economy here. The reindeer came first, in the 1890s, a few years before the gold rush to Nome in 1900. Even before the rush, prospectors were scouring the mountainous peninsula. Today floating dredges still scoop gravel in ponds near Nome and Solomon, while other companies work tin deposits farther west. The reindeer, Native owned exclusively, are thriving, their antlers bringing thousands of dollars when they are sold to Asians for shipment to the Orient.

North of the Seward Peninsula, the Noatak, Kobuk and Selawik rivers enter the Chukchi Sea near Kotzebue. Several Inupiat Eskimo communities dot the Kobuk and Selawik drainages, their residents depending on subsistence and jobs at the Red Dog mine. The Noatak Valley is more pristine, with a solitary village along its lower reaches. Most of the rest of the river lies within Noatak National Preserve.

Sheefish and caribou make up important elements of the region's subsistence economy. The Selawik National Wildlife Refuge was established because of its crucial sheefish spawning habitat. The area is also wintering grounds for the Western Arctic caribou herd.

Other mammals that contribute to the subsistence economy include wolverine, lynx, red fox, river otter, mink, muskrat, beaver, snowshoe hare and wolf. Marten are moving into the area along river valleys, into the Kiana Hills and into a black spruce belt in the Waring Mountains. Black bears and a few grizzlies roam the area, and about 2,000 moose have been counted in the general Kobuk-Selawik region.

About 90 miles north of Kotzebue, Cominco, a Canadian mining company, is taking zinc, lead and silver from Red Dog, which in 1991 yielded 60 percent of U.S.

This slough off the Agulapak River near Lake Nerka in Wood-Tikchik State Park is a haven for ducks and a good place to pick berries. The park embraces a series of fingerlike lakes on the east side of the Wood River Mountains north of Dillingham. (James A. Pickard)

production of zinc, making it one of the world's largest producers of this metal.

Red Dog continues a tradition that has flourished in the region for more than a century. Just as in the Interior, mining has been instrumental in the development of western Alaska, from initial efforts of solitary prospectors to a huge, floating gold dredge offshore at Nome and the open pits at Red Dog.

The desire for furs spawned the first Western settlements in the region at St. Michael, near the mouth of the Yukon, in the 1830s; and at Alexandrovski, near Nushagak, about 1818. Mining took over as an economic force at the turn of the century, when gold was found at Nome. There were also reports of gold up the Kobuk River, near Marshall on the Yukon and at Nyac inland from Bethel. The discovery of platinum near Goodnews Bay in 1926 founded a long-term mine south of Bethel.

Today, Kotzebue, Nome, Bethel and Dillingham are the region's major communities. Each acts as a commercial center for its specific area. Kotzebue revolves around NANA, the Native corporation for northwestern Alaska; the administrative activities of the Northwest Arctic Borough; the Red Dog mine of which NANA is part owner with Cominco; some government jobs including administration of Noatak National Preserve, Krusenstern National Monument and Kobuk Valley National Park in additional to the Selawik National Wildlife Refuge; a small commercial chum salmon run, the northernmost commercial fishery in the state; and subsistence.

Nome serves the southern and western portion of the Seward Peninsula. Its economy depends on mining, mostly small placer operations; government and social service jobs; reindeering and some tourism. Nome is also administrative headquarters for Bering Land Bridge National Preserve, set aside to protect an environment similar to what confronted ancient man when he first crossed the land bridge from Asia to North America.

Bethel, largest community in mainland western Alaska, is the center for the Yup'ik Eskimo people of the Yukon-

Kuskokwim delta, whose population has seen dramatic increases in recent decades with improvement in health care. Bethel depends on subsistence, commercial fishing and on its role as supply center for the many villages spread out around the delta.

Dillingham looks to commercial and sport fishing to sustain its economy. Secondary income comes from tourism, again primarily focused on fishing; government and service sector jobs; and subsistence. Federal staff administer Togiak National Wildlife Refuge from

Largest community on mainland western Alaska, Bethel, population 4,674, lies along the Kuskokwim River and is the trading center for the Yup'ik Eskimo world of the Yukon-Kuskokwim delta. (Staff)

Dillingham, and in summer state rangers oversee spectacular Wood-Tikchik State Park from here.

Southeast of Dillingham, the state narrows into a long, mountainous spine and a chain of islands, the Aleutians.

On the Threshold of Tomorrow:
ALASKA PENINSULA &
ALEUTIAN ISLANDS

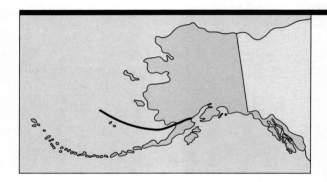

SOUTH OF THE BERING SEA COAST, two of the world's wildest seas lap storm-battered shores of a narrow, mountainous peninsula and a chain of volcanic mountaintops. Alaska's delegate to the circum-Pacific Ring of Fire, the Alaska Peninsula and Aleutian Islands region arcs westward from the south shore of Lake Iliamna more than a thousand miles toward Asia. The treeless Aleutians are actually crests of a 20- to 60-mile-wide ridge of submarine volcanoes that at the summit of Shishaldin Volcano rise 9,372 feet above sea level and 32,472 feet above the ocean floor. Off its Pacific shore, the region is bordered by the Aleutian Trench, a trough more than 2,000 miles long, 50 to 100 miles wide, with a maximum depth of more than 25,000 feet where oceanic and continental tectonic plates collide.

North of the peninsula and island chain, the relatively shallow Bering Sea slopes downward, forming an undersea basin 249 miles long with a maximum depth of 10,677 feet.

There are 124 islands in the Aleutian chain, with chances for more to come as vulcanism propels magma to the top of underwater vents, building up cones whose summits eventually break the ocean's surface to become islands. Weathering then erodes the magma, wearing it down until the island disappears beneath the surface, only to rise again with the next round of volcanic activity. Since the 1700s, Bogoslof Island has appeared, disappeared and reappeared, a specter on the horizon north of Umnak Island.

Residents of the region must contend with another weapon in the Ring of Fire's terrifying arsenal, the earthquake, and its companion, the tsunami or seismic sea wave. Because relatively few people live on the Alaska Peninsula or in the Aleutians, earthquakes here seldom cause substantial losses. But they can generate seismic sea waves of almost incomprehensible fury. On April Fool's Day, 1946, a quake sent a wave more than 100 feet high crashing onto Unimak Island, obliterating Scotch Cap

Volcanic ash up to 700 feet thick covers the Valley of Ten Thousand Smokes in Katmai National Park. The ash is a result of an eruption in June 1912 that deposited incandescent material in a layer at least an inch deep over 30,000 square miles. (Tom Soucek)

Atka, population 87, is certainly one of the most remote communities in Alaska. Residents of this Aleut settlemnent on Atka Island in the central Aleutians live primarily by subsistence, and many Atkans have to leave the island to find work. Archaeological evidence places ancient man at this site at least 2,000 years ago, but the current village was settled in 1860. (Harry M. Walker)

lighthouse and killing five coastguardsmen. The wave then roared south across the Pacific at 500 miles an hour, slamming into Hawaii and killing more than 100 people.

Remnants of past vulcanism clutter the landscape. A quick glance at Aniakchak National Monument and Preserve reveals cinder cones and lava fields collected inside Aniakchak caldera. The volcano last erupted in 1931, but is a reminder of the powerful forces seething beneath the Earth's surface.

A more accessible reminder and certainly one of the region's highlights is Katmai National Park and Preserve and its Valley of Ten Thousand Smokes. Straddling the Aleutian Range south of Lake Iliamna, Katmai gained notoriety in June 1912 when Novarupta and other vents spewed forth more than 6 cubic miles of ash and pumice in the greatest volcanic eruption recorded in Alaska. The eruption prompted the collapse of Mount Katmai and created what came to be called the Valley of Ten Thousand Smokes, a tribute to the hundreds of steam vents puffing from the valley floor when the first scientists inspected the area two years later.

Just as the region's geological history is turbulent, so is

RIGHT: *Typical Aleutian ground cover includes ferns adorned with Kamchatka rhododendrons (dark pink), daisies and wild geraniums (lavender). (Dee Randolph)*

BOTTOM RIGHT: *Among the most common plants on the Alaska Peninsula is the cow parsnip or wild celery, whose buds and stems are edible. Alaska Natives also use parts of the plant for medicines, including as a poultice for wounds and boiled into a tea for sore throats. (Jerg Kroener)*

its weather. Pacific and Bering weather patterns collide in the Aleutians, long known as the birthplace of storms. Sustained winds of 139 mph have whipped across tiny Shemya Island. Measurable precipitation occurs on an average of more than 200 days each year with an annual average of 33 inches at Cold Bay on the Alaska Peninsula and 28 inches at Shemya. Fortunately, temperatures are mild, 40 degrees to 60 degrees in summer and 27 degrees to 37 degrees in winter at Dutch Harbor, the region's largest commercial port.

Marine mammals and seabirds find themselves quite comfortable with the blustery weather. And seemingly unlimited coastal nooks and pinnacles provide plenty of places to nest, pup and rest. There is no lack of food in the nutrient-rich waters surrounding the Aleutians, and all manner of sea-going mammals from giant baleen whales to sea otters and several species of seals cruise the coasts.

Becharof and Alaska Peninsula national wildlife refuges include much of the habitat on the mainland, while Alaska Maritime National Wildlife Refuge protects most of the Aleutian Island habitat. Becharof is known for its high density of brown bears, and for wolves, wolverines, caribou, moose and superb fishing in Becharof Lake and nearby waterways. Alaska Peninsula refuge takes in most of the extremely rugged Pacific coast and its seabird and marine mammal colonies.

At the tip of the peninsula lies Izembek National Wildlife Refuge, home to the world's largest eelgrass beds.

This habitat nourishes almost all of the world's brant and numerous other sea ducks during their staging each fall. Brant gather here to feed and rest before flying south, seemingly en masse, to wintering grounds in Mexico.

While the Alaska Peninsula and Aleutian Islands region has an abundance of wildlife, it is a bit short on people. Aleuts were the prehistoric settlers. Vitus Bering on his 1741 voyage made landfall in the Shumagins, and was shipwrecked on Bering Island, one of the Commander group, the Russian equivalent of the Aleutians. The explorers and traders who followed Bering established posts in the islands before moving on to Kodiak.

By the late 19th century, there were several settlements and outlying fox farms spread throughout the islands. As the 20th century progressed, the bottom fell out of the fur farming industry, and villages were consolidated. By World War II, when the Japanese bombed Unalaska and other islands and U.S. and Japanese forces fought ground battles

FACING PAGE: *Bears are just one of many hazards fish face heading up Brooks Falls to spawning grounds. The short river flows from Brooks Lake over the falls to Naknek Lake in Katmai National Park. The park concessionaire operates Brooks Lodge near the river's mouth, and there is a public campground on Naknek Lake just down the beach from the lodge. Bears roam throughout the area, and it is not uncommon to see several fishermen and bears fishing the river at the same time. (Stephen Rasmussen)*

ABOVE: *Dennis Gearhart shows off a freshly caught silver salmon. Sport and commercial fishing are important ingredients in the economy of the Alaska Peninsula, and visitors come from around the world to fish Brooks River in Katmai National Park. (Tom Soucek)*

RIGHT: *Driftwood litters the beach along Kashvik Bay on the Pacific coast at the extreme southern end of Katmai National Park. Kodiak Island lies about 30 miles across Shelikof Strait, which separates the Alaska Peninsula from the island group. (Tom Soucek)*

FACNG PAGE: *McDonald Cove on the east shore of Agattu Island honors Marshall McDonald, U.S. commissioner of fisheries in the late 1800s. The Near Island group of the Aleutians, those closest to Asia, include Attu, Agattu, and a group of much smaller islands and islets known as the Semichis, of which Shemya Island, location of a U.S. air base, is one. A small contingent of Coast Guardsmen staff a loran station on Attu, site of a furious World War II battle between U.S. and Japanese forces. (Staff)*

ABOVE: *The community of Unalaska and neighboring port of Dutch Harbor are the most important commercial center in the Aleutians. From earliest times, Unalaska Bay has provided sheltered anchorages and thus encouraged settlement along its shores. The Aleuts had villages here, and the Russians established one of their first New World communities at this spot. In recent decades, crabbing and the Bering Sea ground fishery have propelled Dutch Harbor into one of the nation's top ports, ranking first in total tonnage landed and second in value of catch in 1991. (L.J. Campbell)*

on Attu and Kiska islands, the region had only a handful of settlements. It had fewer still after the war, when former residents of Attu were not allowed to move back to their distant village.

Since then, Unalaska and the neighboring port of Dutch Harbor have remained the main commercial center, with

smaller settlements at Atka, Nikolski, Akutan and False Pass. Milt Holmes has lived at Chernofski for most of the past 40 years. Commerce in the Shumagin Islands south of the Alaska Peninsula centers at Sand Point. The rest of the region's Pacific shore has a few small settlements, mostly dependent on subsistence and fishing like Perryville, King Cove and Chignik. Cold Bay was an important military site during World War II and is now the administrative post for Izembek National Wildlife Refuge.

On the Bristol Bay side of the mainland, the administrative center for the peninsula is King Salmon, headquarters for Katmai National Park, and Becharof and

A bull northern fur seal barks at members of his harem on St. Paul Island in the Pribilofs. The islands, in the Bering Sea 200 miles north of the Aleutians, are known for their seabirds and fur seal colonies. (Jo Overholt)

RIGHT: *Unga, focus of Alaska Native activities in the Shumagin Islands, is nestled in the slopes above Delarof Bay on Unga Island. The Shumagin's main settlement is the fishing port of Sand Point on Popof Island. Vitus Bering named the Shumagin Islands, off the south coast of the Alaska Peninsula, for one of his seamen who died on the voyage returning to Kamchatka, Russia in 1741. (Dee Randolph)*

BOTTOM RIGHT: *This castellated headland of Castle Cape runs for 11 miles along the south shore of Castle Bay, 9.5 miles from Chignik on the Alaska Peninsula. Since the Aleutian Range pushes up close to the sea on the Pacific side of the Alaska Peninsula, much of the coastline is a series of convoluted bays backed by rugged, steep-sided mountain slopes. (George Matz)*

Alaska Peninsula refuges. A road connects King Salmon to the fishing port of Naknek; South Naknek lies just across the Naknek River.

Most of the Bristol Bay side of the peninsula is a broad lowland, with plenty of spawning habitat for salmon and other fish. The few settlements scattered along the coast are tied to fish processing facilities, such as at Egegik, Pilot Point and Port Moller.

That is about the best way to sum up the region. From King Salmon to distant Attu, fishing and subsistence rule this rugged tail of Alaska. Unalaska has been the nation's top fishing port more than once. In 1991, the port ranked first in volume of fish landed, 731.7 million pounds, and second in value of catch at $130.6 million for all species. Only the fish actually processed on shore are counted; the activity of floating processors is omitted from these figures. The military bases at Adak and Shemya are the only real exceptions to the fishing economy. There are a few government jobs; some seasonal tourism-related employment, especially at Katmai; and subsistence; but not much else. Perhaps that is the way it should be. In a land as great as Alaska, places unaltered by man seem somehow fitting.

Alaska At A Glance

Alaska has some impressive statistics to go with its Great Land status. Here is a quick look at some of the specifics that make the state so special.

Size: 586,412 square miles; about 365 million acres; one-fifth the size of the contiguous 48 states.

Length of Coastline: 6,640 miles point to point, with a total estimated tidal shoreline of more than 47,000 miles.

BELOW: *This Sitka spruce, Alaska's state tree, stands on the grounds of the Russian Orthodox Church at Seldovia. (Steve McCutcheon)*

RIGHT: *The forget-me-not is Alaska's state flower. (Steve McCutcheon)*

Geographic Center: 63 degrees, 50 minutes north, 152 degrees west; about 60 miles northwest of Mount McKinley near Lake Minchumina.

Northernmost Point: Point Barrow, 71 degrees, 23 minutes north.

Southernmost Point: Amatignak Island, Aleutians, 51 degrees, 13 minutes, five seconds north.

Easternmost and Westernmost Points: Depends on perspective. The 180th meridian is halfway around the world from the prime

meridian at Greenwich, England. The 180th divides east and west and passes through the Aleutians. Therefore, by one perspective, Amatignak Island, 179 degrees, 10 minutes west; and Pochnoi Point, 179 degrees, 46 minutes east are the westernmost and easternmost points respectively. In another view, east is on the right when facing north and west on the left, thus Cape Wrangell on Attu Island, 172 degrees, 27 minutes east is the westernmost point, and Camp Point in southeastern Alaska at 129 degrees, 59 minutes west is the easternmost point.

Time Zones: Two: Alaska Time, one hour behind the West Coast; Hawaii-Aleutian Time, one hour earlier, applies to St. Lawrence Island and the western Aleutians.

Highest Point: Mount McKinley, 20,320 feet; has two peaks, the North Peak is 19,470 feet. In 1909 four sourdoughs from Fairbanks drug a 14-foot log flagpole to the North Peak. In 1913, Rev. Hudson Stuck and his party made first successful climb of South Peak, the true summit. They looked over to the North Peak and saw the spruce flagpole.

Largest Lake: Lake Iliamna, 1,000 square miles.

FACING PAGE: *The two summits of Mount McKinley are visible in this photo looking southwest. The South Peak at left is 20,320 feet, 850 feet higher than the North Peak. (Jon R. Nickles)*

ABOVE: *Alaska's long hours of daylight have produced some giant vegetables such as cabbages and cauliflowers. They have also helped spur a determined effort to establish an agriculture industry, much of which has focused on barley cultivation. After several years of trying, agriculture has yet to become a viable industry, although summer visitors to the Tanana Valley can see acres of barley fields. (Steve McCutcheon)*

RIGHT: *Tlingit elders teach ceremonial dances to younger members of their culture at Sitka. (Steve McCutcheon)*

Longest River: Yukon, 1,400 miles within Alaska

State Bird: Willow Ptarmigan

State Flower: Forget-me-not

State Tree: Sitka Spruce

State Fish: King Salmon

State Fossil: Woolly Mammoth

State Marine Mammal: Bowhead Whale

State Gem: Jade

State Mineral: Gold

State Motto: "North to the Future"

State Flag: Big Dipper and North Star in gold on blue field.

State Song: "Alaska's Flag"

State Capital: Juneau

Native People: Alaska's Natives can be divided into several cultures: the Inupiat Eskimo of the North and Northwest; the Athabaskan Indians of the Interior and upper Cook Inlet; the Yup'ik Eskimos of the West; the Siberian Yup'ks of St. Lawrence Island; the Aleuts of the Alaska Peninsula and Aleutian Islands; people speaking the Eskimo-Aleut Sugpiaq language in parts of the Alaska Peninsula, on Kodiak and around the outer Kenai coast and Prince William Sound; the Eyak Indians of the Cordova area; the Tlingit Indians of Southeast; the Haida Indians of southern Prince of Wales Island; and the Tsimshian of Annette Island.

Daylight Hours:

Summer Maximum

	SUNRISE	SUNSET	HOURS OF DAYLIGHT
Barrow	*	*	*
Fairbanks	12:50 a.m.	10:48 p.m.	21:49 hours
Anchorage	2:21 a.m.	9:42 p.m.	19:21 hours
Juneau	3:51 a.m.	10:09 p.m.	18:18 hours
Ketchikan	4:04 a.m.	9:33 p.m.	17:29 hours
Adak	5:27 a.m.	10:10 p.m.	16:43 hours

Winter Minimum

	SUNRISE	SUNSET	HOURS OF DAYLIGHT
Barrow	*	*	*
Fairbanks	9:59 a.m.	1:41 p.m.	3:42 hours
Anchorage	9:14 a.m.	2:42 p.m.	5:28 hours
Juneau	9:46 a.m.	4:07 p.m.	6:21 hours
Ketchikan	9:12 a.m.	4:18 p.m.	7:06 hours
Adak	9:52 a.m.	5:38 p.m.	7:46 hours

*Note: At Barrow the sun does not set for 84 days (May 10 to Aug. 2), and does not rise for 66 days (Nov. 18 to Jan. 24).

Alaska Populations

UNIFIED HOME RULE MUNICIPALITIES

	7-1-91 POPULATION	APPROX. SQ. MILES	DATE OF INCORPORATION
City and Borough of Juneau	28,965	3,100	July 1, 1970
City and Borough of Sitka	8,588	7,900	Dec. 2, 1971
Municipality of Anchorage	237,907	1,900	Sept. 15, 1975

BOROUGHS

	7-1-91 POPULATION	APPROX. SQ. MILES	DATE OF INCORPORATION
HOME RULE			
Denali Borough	1,783	12,800	Dec. 7, 1990
Lake and Peninsula Borough	1,668	25,000	April 24, 1989
North Slope Borough	8,288	85,000	July 1, 1972
Northwest Arctic Borough	6,113	37,300	June 2, 1986
SECOND CLASS			
Aleutians East Borough	2,464	15,400	Oct. 23, 1987
Bristol Bay Borough	1,410	870	Oct. 2, 1962
Fairbanks North Star Borough	77,720	7,350	Jan. 1, 1964
Kenai Peninsula Borough	40,802	25,600	Jan. 1, 1964
Ketchikan Gateway Borough	13,828	1,250	Sept. 6, 1963
Kodiak Island Borough	15,535	17,800	Sept. 30, 1963
Matanuska-Susitna Borough	41,797	20,550	Jan. 1, 1964
THIRD CLASS			
Haines Borough	2,212	2,600	Aug. 29, 1968

(**Source:** Alaska Department of Community and Regional Affairs)

CITIES

CITY	7-1-91 POPULATION	CITY	7-1-91 POPULATION
Akhiok	77	Anderson	628
Akiak	285	Angoon	690
Akutan	589	Aniak	540
Alakanuk	544	Anvik	82
Aleknagik	185	Atka	87
Allakaket	170	Atmautluak	258
Ambler	311	Atqasuk	216
Anaktuvuk Pass	259	Barrow	3,469

CITY	7-1-91 POPULATION
Bethel	4,674
Bettles	36
Brevig Mission	198
Buckland	318
Chefornak	320
Chevak	598
Chignik	188
Chuathbaluk	97
Clark's Point	60
Coffman Cove	186
Cold Bay	148
Cordova	2,504
Craig	1,637
Deering	157
Delta Junction	736
Dillingham	2,017
Diomede	178
Eagle	168
Eek	284
Ekwok	77
Elim	264
Emmonak	642
Fairbanks	30,843
False Pass	68
Fort Yukon	718
Galena	833
Gambell	525
Golovin	142
Goodnews Bay	241
Grayling	208
Haines	1,265
Holy Cross	277
Homer	3,937
Hoonah	795
Hooper Bay	845
Houston	815
Hughes	66
Huslia	224
Hydaburg	384
Kachemak	365
Kake	700
Kaktovik	224
Kaltag	240
Kasaan	54
Kasigluk	425
Kenai	6,327

CITY	7-1-91 POPULATION
Ketchikan	8,263
Kiana	385
King Cove	811
Kivalina	317
Klawock	758
Kobuk	110
Kodiak	7,229
Kotlik	499
Kotzebue	3,075
Koyuk	253
Koyukuk	126
Kwethluk	558
Larsen Bay	147
Lower Kalskag	300
Manokotak	404
Marshall (Fortuna Ledge)	273
McGrath	528
Mekoryuk	177
Metlakatla	1,469
Mountain Village	674
Napakiak	323
Napaskiak	328
Nenana	504
New Stuyahok	391
Newhalen	160
Newtok	207
Nightmute	153
Nikolai	109
Nome	4,559
Nondalton	178
Noorvik	531
North Pole	1,456
Nuiqsut	354
Nulato	359
Nunapitchuk (Akolmiut)	378
Old Harbor	284
Ouzinkie	209
Palmer	3,008
Pelican	265
Petersburg	3,680
Pilot Point	53
Pilot Station	470
Platinum	64
Point Hope	639

CITY	7-1-91 POPULATION
Port Heiden	119
Port Lions	222
Port Alexander	119
Quinhagak	501
Ruby	170
Russian Mission	246
Saint George	178
Saint Mary's	441
Saint Michael	295
Saint Paul	763
Sand Point	878
Savoonga	545
Saxman	369
Scammon Bay	343
Selawik	596
Seldovia	316
Seward	2,699
Shageluk	139
Shaktoolik	204
Sheldon Point	109
Shishmaref	456
Shungnak	223
Skagway	692
Soldotna	3,482
Stebbins	442
Tanana	407
Teller	151
Tenakee Springs	94
Thorne Bay	569
Togiak	738
Toksook Bay	420
Tuluksak	358
Tununak	316
Unalakleet	714
Unalaska	3,450
Upper Kalskag	172
Valdez	4,360
Wainwright	492
Wales	161
Wasilla	4,028
White Mountain	180
Whittier	279
Wrangell	2,479
Yakutat	534

(**Source:** 1992 Revenue Sharing Program)

Index

ALASKA GEOGRAPHIC® back issues

The North Slope, Vol. 1, No. 1. Charter issue. Out of print.

One Man's Wilderness, Vol. 1, No. 2. Out of print.

Admiralty...Island in Contention, Vol. 1, No. 3. $7.50.

Fisheries of the North Pacific, Vol. 1, No. 4. Out of print.

The Alaska-Yukon Wild Flowers Guide, Vol. 2, No. 1. Out of print.

Richard Harrington's Yukon, Vol. 2, No. 2. Out of print.

Prince William Sound, Vol. 2, No. 3. Out of print.

Yakutat: The Turbulent Crescent, Vol. 2, No. 4. Out of print.

Glacier Bay: Old Ice, New Land, Vol. 3, No. 1. Out of print.

The Land: Eye of the Storm, Vol. 3, No. 2. Out of print.

Richard Harrington's Antarctic, Vol. 3, No. 3. $12.95.

The Silver Years of the Alaska Canned Salmon Industry: An Album of Historical Photos, Vol. 3, No. 4. $17.95.

Alaska's Volcanoes: Northern Link In the Ring of Fire, Vol. 4, No. 1. Out of print.

The Brooks Range, Vol. 4, No. 2. Out of print.

Kodiak: Island of Change, Vol. 4, No. 3. Out of print.

Wilderness Proposals, Vol. 4, No. 4. Out of print.

Cook Inlet Country, Vol. 5, No. 1. Out of print.

Southeast: Alaska's Panhandle, Vol. 5, No. 2. Out of print.

Bristol Bay Basin, Vol. 5, No. 3. Out of print.

Alaska Whales and Whaling, Vol. 5, No. 4. $19.95.

Yukon-Kuskokwim Delta, Vol. 6, No. 1. Out of print.

Aurora Borealis, Vol. 6, No. 2. $14.95.

Alaska's Native People, Vol. 6, No. 3. $24.95.

The Stikine River, Vol. 6, No. 4. $12.95.

Alaska's Great Interior, Vol. 7, No. 1. $17.95.

A Photographic Geography of Alaska, Vol. 7, No. 2. $17.95.

The Aleutians, Vol. 7, No. 3. $19.95.

Klondike Lost: A Decade of Photographs by Kinsey & Kinsey, Vol. 7, No. 4. Out of print.

Wrangell-Saint Elias, Vol. 8, No. 1. $19.95.

Alaska Mammals, Vol. 8, No. 2. $15.95.

The Kotzebue Basin, Vol. 8, No. 3. $15.95.

Alaska National Interest Lands, Vol. 8, No. 4. $17.95.

Alaska's Glaciers, Vol. 9, No. 1. Out of print.

Sitka and Its Ocean/Island World, Vol. 9, No. 2. $19.95.

Islands of the Seals: The Pribilofs, Vol. 9, No. 3. $12.95.

Alaska's Oil/Gas & Minerals Industry, Vol. 9, No. 4. $15.95.

Adventure Roads North, Vol. 10, No. 1. $17.95.

Anchorage and the Cook Inlet Basin, Vol. 10, No. 2. $17.95.

Alaska's Salmon Fisheries, Vol. 10, No. 3. $15.95.

Up the Koyukuk, Vol. 10, No. 4. $17.95.

Nome: City of the Golden Beaches, Vol. 11, No. 1. $14.95.

Alaska's Farms and Gardens, Vol. 11, No. 2. $15.95.

Chilkat River Valley, Vol. 11, No. 3. $15.95.

Alaska Steam, Vol. 11, No. 4. $14.95.

Northwest Territories, Vol. 12, No. 1. $17.95.

Alaska's Forest Resources, Vol. 12, No. 2. $16.95.

Alaska Native Arts and Crafts, Vol. 12, No. 3. $17.95.

Our Arctic Year, Vol. 12, No. 4. $15.95.

Where Mountains Meet the Sea: Alaska's Gulf Coast, Vol. 13, No. 1. $17.95.

Backcountry Alaska, Vol. 13, No. 2. $17.95.

British Columbia's Coast, Vol. 13, No. 3. $17.95.

Lake Clark/Lake Iliamna Country, Vol. 13, No. 4. Out of print.

Dogs of the North, Vol. 14, No. 1. $17.95.

South/Southeast Alaska, Vol. 14, No. 2. Out of print.

Alaska's Seward Peninsula, Vol. 14, No. 3. $15.95.

The Upper Yukon Basin, Vol. 14, No. 4. $17.95.

Glacier Bay: Icy Wilderness, Vol. 15, No. 1. Out of print.

Dawson City, Vol. 15, No. 2. $15.95.

Denali, Vol. 15, No. 3. $16.95.

The Kuskokwim River, Vol. 15, No. 4. $17.95.

Katmai Country, Vol. 16, No. 1. $17.95.

North Slope Now, Vol. 16, No. 2. $14.95.

The Tanana Basin, Vol. 16, No. 3. $17.95.

The Copper Trail, Vol. 16, No. 4. $17.95.

The Nushagak Basin, Vol. 17, No. 1. $17.95.

Juneau, Vol. 17, No. 2. $17.95.

The Middle Yukon River, Vol. 17, No. 3. $17.95.

The Lower Yukon River, Vol. 17, No. 4. $17.95.

Alaska's Weather, Vol. 18, No. 1. $17.95.

Alaska's Volcanoes, Vol. 18, No. 2. $17.95.

Admiralty Island: Fortress of the Bears, Vol. 18, No. 3. $17.95.

Unalaska/Dutch Harbor, Vol. 18, No. 4. $17.95.

Skagway: A Legacy of Gold, Vol. 19, No. 1. $18.95.

ALL PRICES SUBJECT TO CHANGE.

Your $39 membership in The Alaska Geographic Society includes four subsequent issues of *ALASKA GEOGRAPHIC*®, the Society's official quarterly. Please add $10 for non-U.S. memberships.

Additional membership information is available upon request. Single copies of the *ALASKA GEOGRAPHIC*® back issues are also available. When ordering, please make payments in U.S. funds and add $2.00 postage/handling per copy book rate; $4.00 per copy for Priority mail. Non-U.S. postage extra. To order back issues send your check or money order and volumes desired to:

The Alaska Geographic Society

P.O. Box 93370
Anchorage, AK 99509

NEXT ISSUE: *Kodiak*, Vol. 19, No. 3. One of Alaska's largest communities, some of its fiercest wildlife, its most rugged wilderness and wildest waters make up the Kodiak archipelago, that string of islands that flank the western side of the Gulf of Alaska. This issue will take a look at the area's history, commerce, lifestyle and environment. To members 1992, with index $18.95.

Changes Afloat in Alaska's Commercial Fisheries

By L.J. Campbell

Alaska's coastal communities are anxiously tracking new federal proposals that would further regulate commercial fishing. The proposals, if made into law, will change the way people live and do business in Alaska's coastal fishing towns.

In Unalaska, home to Dutch Harbor, the nation's leading fishing port in tonnage landed, arguments about pollock allocations between onshore and offshore processors disrupt city council meetings. In Kodiak, Alaska's busiest fishing port for the Gulf of Alaska fleet, people predict the demise of small commercial fishermen should IFQs, or individual fishing quotas, go into effect for halibut and black cod.

And in Anchorage, a group of cannery owners, fishermen, biologists and economists hold another monthly meeting to debate the ABCs of fishing, as well as the TACs, DAPs and DAHs. Discussions by this group, the North Pacific Fishery Management Council, are plugged with acronyms — such as acceptable biological catch (ABC), total

allowable catch (TAC), domestic annual processing (DAP), and domestic annual harvest (DAH) — key concepts in the complicated regulatory world of commercial fishing.

Commercial fishing these days is as much a paper chase as a race to

fill the nets. Fishermen today must keep up with a growing number of government rules. The regulations have dual goals: to keep a healthy number of fish in the ocean and to maximize economic benefits to the fishing industry. It is a tall order. Fish populations fluctuate for

Crewmen work the trawl deck during the pollock fishery in the Gulf of Alaska. (Marion Stirrup)

many reasons — among them, changing water temperatures, availability of food, pollution and

The oil-rich sablefish (Anoplopoma fimbria), is often marketed as black cod, even though it is not a true cod. Commercial longlining of sablefish in Alaska started in Southeast in 1906; rapid growth of the fishery during the last decade has resulted in ever-shortening seasons that are approaching 24-hour derbies. Predominantly taken by longliners, sablefish is the third largest Gulf of Alaska fishery in total tonnage, behind pollock and Pacific cod. Its high value, however, is rivaled only by halibut. Most U.S. sablefish is sold in Japan, where it is a traditional wintertime food. (National Marine Fisheries Service)

overfishing by humans. Maintaining a healthy ocean ecosystem is an imprecise science at best, and controlling the human impact is part of that.

Rulemakers try to prevent overfishing by limiting the harvest with such methods as catch quotas and gear restrictions, or by limiting the number of fishermen, or a combination of both. At stake is one of Alaska's larger basic industries. On a personal level the regulations can be bewildering, frustrating and time-consuming.

A number of government agencies — including the federal North Pacific Fishery Management Council and the Alaska Department of Fish and Game — are involved in regulating Alaska's various fisheries. Generally, the state manages fishing in Alaska's rivers and nearshore ocean waters, up to three miles from land, and the North Pacific Fishery Management Council regulates fisheries in Alaska's offshore waters three miles to 200 miles from land.

But because fish migrate, the responsibilities of the regulatory agencies overlap. For instance, the North Pacific Fishery Management Council's primary focus is managing the groundfish fisheries — nearly a dozen commercially valuable species including pollock, cod, soles, flounders, sablefish, rockfish and perch. Decisions made by the 15-member council are subject to approval by the U.S. Secretary of Commerce. The National Marine Fisheries Service augments the council, serving as its primary research arm and conducting programs to support council directives. But in addition to regulating the groundfish fishery, the council works with the Alaska Department of Fish and Game's Board of Fisheries to oversee crab and herring fisheries, and it cooperates with the International Pacific Halibut Commission to regulate halibut fishing. At the same time, while regulation of commercial salmon fishing falls to Alaska's Department of Fish and Game, the council works to limit the amount of salmon accidentally caught in the groundfish and high seas drift net fisheries.

From this regulatory maze come rules on when, where, how long and how deep fishermen may fish; what type of gear and size of boat they can use; the type, size and amount of fish they may catch; and who may do the fishing.

Alaska's fisheries have been regulated to some degree for more than a century — federal control of salmon fishing to protect commercial salteries and canneries began as early as 1896. Statehood generated a new bureaucracy, and in the last 20 years the number and complexity of fishing laws have snowballed, beginning with introduction of the limited entry permit system for salmon in 1973. Keeping up with requirements, changes and proposed changes in Alaska's various fisheries can be nearly a full-time job, particularly for those who engage in more than one. Participating in multiple fisheries is a common way for fishermen to maximize their investments in boats and gears. Commercial fishermen these days are likely to fill up their calendars with one opening after another.

For instance, in Kodiak, home port to a large commercial salmon fleet, fishermen often participate in crab, herring, pollock and cod fisheries that flank the four-month-long summer salmon season. All the while, they must stay alert to news of closings in certain areas of the ocean or other developments. At any time, the council may shut down a fishery in a specific area or for a type of gear. The council may do this if the total catch of the targeted fish or the accidental catch of other fish reaches predetermined levels.

In the meantime, trained individuals called observers are on board a number of boats, noting the size, type and tonnage of fish or crabs being caught. They report back to the National Marine Fisheries Service, which uses observer information and weekly catch reports filed by each vessel to advise the council about current fishing activity.

Subsistence and sport fishing in Alaska each have their own rules, and conflicts exist between subsistence, sport and commercial fisheries. What follows, however, provides a closer look at two current regulatory debates in Alaska's commercial fisheries.

Quotas and Allocations

Anytime commercial fishermen in Alaska's coastal communities get together these days, their conversations soon turn to such things as individual fishing quotas and pollock allocations — two of the more controversial proposals ever advanced by the North Pacific Fishery Management Council.

The council was created 16 years ago, one of eight regional fishery management councils to oversee the 1976 Magnuson Fishery Conservation and Management Act. The North Pacific council covers fisheries of the Arctic Ocean, Bering and Chukchi seas, and the Pacific Ocean seaward of Alaska; the other seven councils have jurisdiction in other U.S. coastal waters.

Part of the council's role is establishing annual harvest guidelines for groundfish. Among other things, the council also sets yearly limits for bycatch, or incidental harvest of fish other than the targeted species. Bycatch is a troubling aspect of the commercial fisheries occurring with all gear types, but particularly associated with the indiscriminate nature of huge trawler nets and drift nets that scoop up many forms of sealife. Harvest quotas and bycatch limits together add up to the total catch allowed, an amount biologists think can be removed without harming stocks. Monitoring the harvest presents a list of other challenges. The council's management plans are complicated and lengthy; the Bering Sea/Aleutian Islands Groundfish Fishery Management Plan alone is 29 pages.

The Magnuson Act that created the council opened a new era for commercial fisheries. Prior to the 1980s, the groundfish fisheries — primarily pollock and cod — off Alaska's coast were dominated by foreign fleets. The Magnuson Act gradually phased out the foreign fleet, promoting expansion of the domestic fishing industry to harvest and process the groundfish. By 1990, the groundfish fishery in waters three to 200 miles from Alaska's shore had been fully "Americanized."

But on the way to Americanization, something unanticipated happened. The U.S. fishing fleet grew faster than expected — from no factory trawlers in 1980 to a fleet of 64 ships by 1991. Growth in the shore-based seafood processing plants was equally astounding. New processing plants sprang up in places like Dutch Harbor and Kodiak, and existing plants were expanded. The growth on and offshore was bought with money from U.S. companies as well as those from Japan, Korea and Norway.

Now the council estimates that to keep every boat and processing line operating to full capacity, the floating and shore-based processors need more than twice the current

*Pollock (*Theragra chalcogramma*), the most abundant groundfish in the Bering Sea, is the target of fierce competition between factory trawlers and onshore processors. Although it is a relatively low-value fish, its total tonnage makes it the largest groundfish fishery in the Bering Sea and Gulf of Alaska. Caught mostly by midwater trawl gear, its white flesh is processed as fillets and made into surimi, commonly sold as artificial crab. (National Marine Fisheries Service)*

pollock and Pacific cod quota (1.82 million metric tons in 1991). Such overcapitalization has heightened competition as each group scrambles to get enough fish.

This competition erupted in 1989 when offshore factory trawler vessels moved into the Gulf of Alaska. The offshore trawlers that year harvested half the total pollock quota, which significantly cut the amount the shore-based processors anticipated receiving. The previous year, trawlers had taken less than 15 percent of the quota. Fishermen and processors from Kodiak asked the North Pacific council to allocate the quota between the onshore and offshore interests, to prevent the offshore trawlers from preempting the onshore processors. The shore-based interests implored the council to not ignore the social and economic importance of a steady supply of fish to coastal communities.

The council studied the situation in the Gulf of Alaska and the Bering Sea/Aleutian Islands

Workers hand sort flatfish fillets at the All Alaskan Seafoods plant at Kodiak. The groundfish fisheries, primarily pollock and cod, were dominated by foreign fleets prior to the 1980s. The Magnuson Fishery Conservation and Management Act gradually changed the complexion of the groundfishery by promoting domestic participation. (Marion Stirrup)

management districts. It developed several alternatives to address the preemption issue. In the meantime, the council portioned the annual pollock catch into quarterly quotas. The quarterly quotas effectively dampened trawler interest in the Gulf pollock fishery, which at an annual total of 133,400 metric tons is small compared to the Bering Sea pollock quota of 1.3 million metric tons. In 1990 and 1991 after the quarterly quotas were imposed, the trawlers processed around 20 percent of the Gulf pollock quota, down considerably from their take in 1989.

In June 1991, the council adopted two proposals for pollock

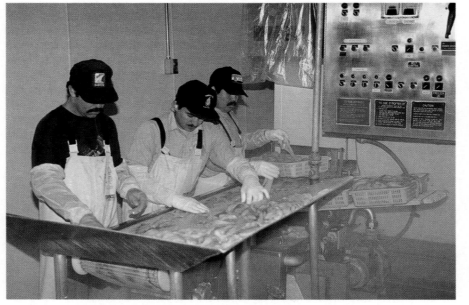

allocations between onshore and offshore processors. The proposal for Bering Sea pollock gave 35 percent to onshore processors and 65 percent to offshore processors in 1992, with the allocation for the onshore segment increasing to 40 percent in 1993 and to 45 percent in 1994. The council's proposal for the Gulf of Alaska allocated 100 percent of the pollock and 90 percent of the Pacific cod to onshore processors for 1992 through 1994.

On March 5, 1992, Undersecretary for Oceans and Atmosphere John A. Knauss approved the council's Gulf plan for all three years, but approved only the 1992 allocation for the Bering Sea. The approved

allocations are expected to take effect the last half of 1992. But debate on the issue continues. The council is looking at alternative Bering Sea pollock allocation proposals for 1993 and 1994 to offer to the Secretary of Commerce, probably by August 1992. At the same time, the council is trying to decide a related issue: How to allocate the bycatch of prohibited species — halibut, crab and salmon — between the onshore/offshore groups.

The approved allocation plan also included a pollock allocation for Alaska fishing communities to encourage development of groundfishery economy. This "community development quota" sets aside 7.5 percent of the total Bering Sea quota for harvest by eligible communities. The state of Alaska is now developing the eligibility criteria and deciding how much each community will get.

Meanwhile, the American Factory Trawler Association says it may challenge the allocation decision in court.

The Allocation Controversy

At stake in the allocation proposals is the North Pacific bottomfish harvest — most of which is pollock worth $1 billion a year. The competitors are the onshore and offshore processors. The onshore processors comprise 19 seafood processing plants and around 160 boats that deliver to them. The onshore processors include Alaska-owned plants but increasingly are dominated by larger foreign-owned processors that have made considerable investments in Alaska during the past several years. The offshore group includes trawling vessels with processing facilities on board, vessels called motherships that are giant floating processors only, and the catcher boats that deliver to them. The offshore fleet historically has harvested 75 to 80 percent of the Bering Sea pollock catch.

The allocation plan was designed by the council to protect onshore processors from preemption by the offshore processors. The plan will primarily benefit the shore-based catchers and processors and their local port communities. The benefits include increased or stabilized incomes, employment and related economic activity, according to council analyses. The allocation likewise will mean less fish for the offshore fleet and that means economic ills for the offshore operations, their supporting service industries and communities. While the factory trawler fleet is mostly based in Seattle, the ships do considerable business when in Alaska ports during the fishing season.

The Bering Sea allocation proposal has initiated considerable controversy in the Aleutian Island fishing town of Unalaska, for

Pacific cod spill from the net into the hold of a factory trawler. (National Marine Fisheries Service)

instance, where both segments play heavily into its economy. The town has seven onshore processors, including three huge plants built in the past four years to turn pollock into surimi, which is commonly sold in the United States as artificial crabmeat. At the same time, Unalaska's Port of Dutch Harbor has added docks, and fishing support businesses have expanded to meet the demands of the Bering Sea factory trawler fleet.

In reviewing the council's proposals, the Commerce Department's inspector general criticized the Bering Sea plan because it did not address the problem of overcapitalization, among other things. Nor did it

solve the problem of processing overcapacity, or address competition that may arise within each group.

The loudest outcry against the council's plan has come from the American Factory Trawler Association based in Seattle. It represents the North Pacific fleet with boats ranging from 100 feet to 600 feet in length and designed to produce surimi for export or fillet blocks. The fleet follows the fish, processing continually and staying at sea for weeks at a time. Trawlers are capable of harvesting more than 50,000 metric tons a year. When fishing slows or is closed in one area, they move to another area or into the unregulated high

seas. A typical factory trawler is a 275-foot vessel valued at more than $30 million with some $10 million in onboard processing equipment and a crew of more than 50. One vessel can produce $25 million in seafood annually.

The association and shipowners say the allocation system punishes them for doing what the Magnuson Act encouraged: investing to develop the groundfish fishery. The allocation plan, they say, will bankrupt shipowners, costing hundreds of jobs in the factory trawler fleet. They argue that fish processed and flash frozen at sea within hours of being caught is fresher and of better quality for the consumer than fish processed on shore. The trawler association complains that the council is stacked with members who favor Alaska's shore-based industry and want to "Alaskanize" the fishery, therefore the council's analyses are skewed and faulty.

On the opposite side, supporters of preferential onshore allocations say the shore-based plants cannot move to follow the fish and need a steady supply to continue operating. In the long-term, they say, the shore-based industry contributes more taxes — local and

A salmon seiner is underway in Marmot Bay near Kodiak. The commercial salmon industry has been regulated by limited entry for nearly two decades. (Marion Stirrup)

Individual Fishing Quotas

Alaska's commercial fishermen also are watching the council's proposal to divvy the quota of sablefish (black cod) and halibut among fishermen by assigning individual fishery quotas, or IFQs. Although the proposal currently applies to only fixed-gear halibut and sablefish fisheries, the council has indicated it may extend IFQs to pollock and Pacific cod fisheries.

The sablefish fishery supports the largest fleet and feeds more processors than any other groundfish fishery in the North Pacific. The majority of sablefish processors are in Southeast Alaska. Sablefish also bring the highest ex-vessel price of any groundfish. Growth in the fishery has surged in the past decade, and efforts to control the fishery have been underway since 1985 when the council began restricting gear types to hook and line. Limited entry was the management alternative favored by a majority of longliners, according to a 1987 survey by the North Pacific Longline Coalition. Although a limited entry license program was explored as an alternative by the council, it chose

state raw fish tax, property tax and income tax on profits — than the factory fleet which usually pays only state fuel taxes and local sales taxes.

Each side complains that the other is financed by foreign interests that want control of the

fisheries. The biggest shore-based plants processing groundfish in Dutch Harbor, for instance, are owned by two of Japan's largest seafood companies, Nippon Suisan and Taiyo. The trawler association says that guaranteeing these shore-based processors a percentage of

the catch amounts to giving them market control. Yet the trawler fleet has significant foreign investors as well; a General Accounting Office report found 30 percent of the factory fleet was built or rebuilt in Norway, Japan or Korea.

instead to go with individual fishing quotas.

Fishermen would qualify for IFQs based on their past history in the fishery. Boat owners and crew members who meet the council's qualifications would be assigned quota shares.

The plan allows buying, selling and leasing of IFQs. No one person would be allowed to own, hold or control more than 1 percent of the combined total for any management area (Gulf of Alaska, Bering Sea/Aleutian Islands, East Yakutat and Southeast Outside), or more than 0.5 percent of the total for combined management areas.

Under IFQs, fishermen would have the entire year to catch and deliver their quota, rather than the current limited openings. Supporters of IFQs say the system would provide fresh fish throughout the year. With IFQs, they say, fishermen would have more control and could fish in optimal weather, not subjected to the frenzied, crowded and dangerous fishing that characterize, for instance, the 24-hour halibut derbies. Gear conflicts — such as setting lines on top of others that occur in crowded waters — would be reduced and this would probably mean less deadloss from abandoned gear.

Some feel the IFQs are a partial answer to the bycatch mortality problem. With IFQs, fishermen could land some of their quota as bycatch in other fisheries, and this would decrease the amount of sablefish and halibut wasted. Even though those who do not hold IFQs would have to discard all their sablefish and halibut bycatch, the result might still be a decrease in bycatch mortality, according to the council, since fewer boats would have to worry about it.

Those against IFQs say it amounts to a class system favoring the wealthy who will buy up the shares. In a decade, the price of IFQs will skyrocket, effectively shutting out young and less well-financed fishermen and essentially changing the social make-up of local fishing communities, they predict. Objectors also say IFQs would mean less income for fishing crews. Experienced crews now command premium wages; the better the crew the more likely a boat will maximize its catch during a short opening. Since IFQs would allow fishing throughout the year, the skill and speed of the crew might not matter as much.

Alaska's fisheries historically have been managed for open access. In a fishery open to all fishermen, harvesting capacity is managed by controlling the fishermen with catch, gear and area allocations and quotas by area, gear type and species. Another way of managing fisheries is limiting access: This first occurred in Alaska with the limited entry permit program for salmon fishermen and now 45 of the state's 200 or so fisheries — including the 27 salmon fisheries, eight herring fisheries, three black cod fisheries and seven crab fisheries — are under limited entry.

The IFQ system would be similar, but with a kicker. Limited entry salmon permits only give fishermen the right to fish. IFQs go another step by guaranteeing a percentage of the quota. Therefore, IFQ opponents reason, IFQs will command higher selling prices than salmon permits.

The limited entry salmon program has been criticized for shutting people out of the fishery because of high permit prices; a seine permit for the rich Chignik red salmon fishery sold for $500,000 in 1992 and in the Bristol Bay sockeye fishery, drift net permits bring $175,000.

The council considered this phenomenon — sometimes called the "permit drain" — in drafting its IFQ proposal. The proposal includes "community quotas" for qualified western Alaska communities.

In August 1992, the Secretary of Commerce is expected to receive the council's final halibut and sablefish IFQ proposal — which includes comments gathered during a 45-day public review period in May and June 1992. If approved, the plan will go into effect in 1994.

An Earthshaking Event, 1964

By Michael V. McGee

Editor's note: *Most Alaskans know about the tremendous jolt that shook Southcentral Alaska on Good Friday, 1964. Michael McGee of North Pole gives this account of his experiences with the great quake. McGee's parents both worked for newspapers, and he lived several places in the Midwest and South before settling in Tennessee where he earned a law degree. Most of his work career was spent with the U.S. Air Force, which sent him to Alaska first in 1962. He returned in 1972 to Eielson Air Force Base in Fairbanks. McGee says that when he could no longer extend his tour in Alaska, he retired as a major in 1979 so he could remain in the state.*

Large cracks opened along Fourth Avenue in downtown Anchorage as land on the north side sloughed downhill toward Ship Creek. (Office of 11th Air Force)

I spent the Great Alaska Earthquake in a bar. The bar was located in the basement of the Officers Club at Elmendorf Air Force Base in Anchorage. I was there because, besides being Good Friday, it was Tom Shepherd's birthday, and he had invited all squadron officers to have a martini in celebration. He was buying.

I had been stationed at Elmendorf for a little more than a year, having been reassigned from a radar site in Wisconsin. The radar site had been manned by about a hundred people. Elmendorf had about 6,000, plus civilian employees, plus dependents; moreover, it adjoined the Army's Fort Richardson, which was about the same size. Anchorage then had a population of about 50,000. You might say the military dominated Anchorage.

Elmendorf, headquarters of the Alaskan Command, was the hub of the outer defense line of the United States. Because of this frontline atmosphere and its remoteness from the "real world," there was some relaxation of formal military discipline and an emphasis on esprit de corps. You might get by missing a salute if you were wearing your squadron's colors and singing the Air Force song.

The Anchorage area, in fact all southern Alaska, constantly rattles with small earthquakes. The number and strength of these small rattles had increased noticeably since Christmas — nothing damaging, just unsettling.

Everyone went through a social custom, a routine, during these quake-ettes. The women became feminine, got bug-eyed, gave little gasps and ohs and clutched the nearest male hand or arm. If there were no available males, they clutched their purses. The men meanwhile became macho, got steely eyed, and made calm but forceful statements like, "It's all right," or "It'll quit in a minute." They were always right; it always quit in a few seconds.

On March 27, 1964, at 5:37 p.m., in the basement bar of the Officers' Club, women were going, "oh," and several men were going, "It's all right," but it did not quit, and some said, "Oh, oh!"

It is instinctive to get out of buildings during a strong earthquake, and when the room gave a sudden lurch that toppled empty chairs and knocked bottles and glasses from the bar and tables, most everyone stood, or tried to. The lights went out; it was pitch black in the basement as people scrambled for the stairway. I stepped on a bottle just as the room lurched again, and went down on the floor in a pile of broken glass.

I tried to stand; someone fell over me and knocked me back. I found a table leg and crawled under the table because I was afraid the building would collapse. Some reached the stairs but were thrown back when they tried to climb. Only two or three actually made it outside. The last of these was Tom Shepherd. He left the outside door open, so a little light penetrated to the basement down the winding stairway.

He was the last to make it out because the quake intensified. Even crawling was impossible. The floor went up and down till our stomachs reacted like in a fast elevator. The floor went back and forth, and tilted and skewered like some fun machine at the fair. It jolted like driving off a curb. But overall there was a pattern to it: a movement to the left and a rise, a fall and a movement to the right, and another rise, like being on the end of a bouncing pendulum. There was a woman under the table with me. When the ground moved to the left, she took a breath; when it moved to the right, she screamed. I could hardly hear her over the roaring and grinding that accompanied the earth

A portion of Bluff Road on Elmendorf Air Force Base slipped down during the 1964 Good Friday earthquake. (Office of 11th Air Force)

movement, but the pattern of her screams indicated the pattern of the movement.

The quake lasted an estimated five to seven minutes. No one ever thinks to look at his watch during such an event, but however long it lasted, the time seemed interminable. The quake finally stopped, with a tremendous bump as if the whole building had fallen eight or 10 feet. The roaring stopped, and everything was quiet. Someone asked, "Anyone hurt?" But remarkably no one was. People began to rush up the stairway and out.

It was still winter outside and I

wanted my coat and car keys, so I did not go with the crowd. Instead, I went up another stairway that led to the coat rack on the first floor. I got my coat and stepped outside into the parking lot.

I had expected to see everything in shambles, but at first most things appeared perfectly normal — with a few exceptions. Most of the exceptions were people. They lay scattered around the partly snowy ground like corpses in a battle movie. Two men lay head to head, grasping each other's shoulders like wrestlers. Another man, a friend, still stood, feet spread wide apart, bent way over

and clinging to the metal pole of a stop sign. The cars in the lot had sustained little damage. A few had rolled into odd positions. All the rest had skidded around and lined up neatly so that they were headed across the yellow parking lines instead of sitting parallel between them. The friend at the stop sign later told me he had strained to stand so he could watch the ground move in oceanlike waves across the open land by the club, and the cars dance in unison across the lot. He had been slung around so much that the sign pole was bent. For months afterwards the parking lot was covered with hundreds of skid marks.

Since I was concerned about my family, I started my car and headed off base. Not another car was moving, but I could not drive fast because I passed so many that had just stopped where they were, the drivers still sitting in them, staring. The guard at the gate was outside his guard box, staring at it as I went by. He did not see me.

I should emphasize that I was driving slowly. My only prior experience with large earthquakes was in seeing the movie "One Million B.C." in which giant fissures opened to swallow dinosaurs. I was so busy watching for big fissures I drove right across one 2 inches to 3 inches wide in front of our house, from which escaped a strong sulfurous odor.

A block away this crack widened

The Government Hill Elementary School was left a twisted mass of steel and wood after the March 27, 1964 earthquake. School was not in session on Good Friday, but when the children did return to class, they had to be double shifted at those schools still in operation. (Office of 11th Air Force)

to a foot and then went across town slowly widening until in downtown Anchorage cars and buildings had fallen into it. Then it turned south and headed into Turnagain and destroyed that wealthy subdivision. A movie theater in downtown Anchorage had sunk so far its marquee sat on the ground.

My apartment was in pretty good shape except that many nails had been pulled at the corners of interior walls, and I could see where the walls had rubbed against each other for several inches. Our furniture and personal property had been thrown about, and things

were a mess, but damage was light. A turtle had disappeared from its bowl. Outside, my kids were rebuilding a snowman. No one was hurt.

I drove back on the base. Most cars were still not moving. I stopped by the squadron barracks. No one was injured there, although in an adjoining barracks a man had broken a leg when he panicked and jumped out a second-story window. He had been the only one seriously injured at Elmendorf.

I loaded my car with members of my squadron, and we drove on to the hangars. Damage to the

airplanes was severe. The hangars had heavy overhead lights fastened to supporting eyes with S-hooks. The swinging of these lights had been enough to dislodge the hooks, and the falling lights had bombed the planes, plunging right through wings and fuselages. Somehow the mechanics working in the hangars had escaped injury.

On the base, major structural damage had been limited to two collapsed warehouses and several buildings that had to be temporarily evacuated. The largest of these was the seven-story hospital. A coin dropped on the top floor in one place would land in the basement. The patients took unexpected and often painful trips on their wheeled beds as the building swayed and shoved them from wall to wall.

Damage to Anchorage was much more severe and has been well documented. The human stories were most interesting. Penney's department store had been virtually destroyed. Two boys found trapped in an elevator in Penney's had been jumping and

making it bounce when the quake started. When they were released, they apologized hysterically for all the damage they had caused.

People in the streets formed chains and held hands so they would not fall into the fissures. One man running naked from a Turkish bath had each of his arms grabbed and held in one long chain. He later figured he had enough exposure to run for public office. He was elected.

Some people lost all contact with reality. The lady who lived next door had just taken a disaster survival course. Immediately after the motion stopped, she went trancelike to the bathroom, dipped the baby's bottle in the toilet holding tank, filled it about two-thirds full, then filled the rest with chlorine bleach. She woke the baby and gave it a drink. The baby was sick but survived. She was a doctor's wife with fresh water still in her refrigerator. Another neighbor, just moving in, demanded to know, "Does this happen all the time?"

A two-year-old, sitting on a potty chair when the quake started, found himself skittering wildly across the floor, and commanded over and over, "Whoa, house!"

A flight surgeon being given informal flying lessons aboard an Air Force plane was coming in for a landing. When all the radios went dead on final approach, he assumed he had broken the airplane. The regular pilot aborted the landing and flew around, but he could not get any reply on the radio nor any other signals from the tower. The world seemed to have disappeared. With fuel getting low, he finally landed and found that the concrete runway in places had turned to gravel. His plane was immediately taken over by tower personnel who used it as a control tower. For several hours, Elmendorf had the only fully functional airport in that part of the state.

A man in Turnagain had been practicing his trumpet. He ran outside in a panic and fell into a developing sink hole. Dirt began filling the hole, and he could not climb out because he could not pull his buried arm out of the rubble. Finally he remembered to let go of his trumpet, and he pulled his arm free and climbed to safety.

A G.I. in a paint warehouse tried to clean up six inches of spilled paint on the floor with a mop and broom.

Many people fled. A young lady taking the first flight available ended up in Tokyo, with no passport, no money, no baggage.

Shortly after motion stopped, the radios began to come back on with emergency generators, and mukluk telegraph — informal announcements of personal news to Bush residents still in use today — became the standard mode of broadcast:

A backhoe is needed on Fourth Avenue near the bridge. Anyone who can get through with a backhoe is requested to do so. All nurses are to report to their hospital. All unemployed practical and private nurses are requested to report to the Red Cross or to Providence Hospital. All military personnel will report to their units. We have unconfirmed reports that Valdez and Kodiak have been hit with tidal waves and that Seward is burning. Tidal waves are expected in the Anchorage area within the next four hours. Everyone stay away from the shore area. It is reported there are several inches of spilled oil and gasoline along the shore. No smoking, repeat, no smoking at all in the shore area. A bulldozer is needed immediately in the area of L Street Apartments. Do not try to drive out of the city as all roads are blocked, and most service stations cannot pump gas due to the general electric failure. Electricity is expected to be restored to the downtown area by morning, but everyone is encouraged to boil their drinking water until further notice. All aircraft are restricted from flying over the city since the vibration is causing further damage. Aftershocks can be expected for several days but are not expected to be as severe as the original quake. All public utility employees and telephone employees are requested to report to their job. There is an estimated 30-days supply of food in the city. Hoarding is not necessary. The Red Cross needs blood. You may

contribute at the Red Cross Headquarters or any hospital. We will stay on the air continuously until the emergency is over. Personal messages will be relayed as time permits. Our phones are out, and messages should be brought directly to the station. To anyone at Unalakleet: Rosie is okay. To Bob and Terrel at Rampart: We are all right, but cannot get out of Anchorage, please feed the dogs, Judy. To Carl at King Salmon: Tell Mom we are okay, just shook up, Jerry.

The messages at first were jerky, staccato, unprofessional. Yet they calmed the people and got the job done. Music and top tunes disappeared for a couple of days, except when announcers, who were frequently working alone, had to take a break.

Gradually things returned to normal, although utilities were off in some sections of the city for a month or more, and National Guardsmen patrolled the devastated areas, weapons loaded. Slowly rubble was cleared, old buildings repaired or demolished, and new ones built, giving Anchorage its new skyline.

On base, the hospital was

repaired, the phones fixed, the paint cleaned up, the Officers' Club reopened, but not the basement bar. Before the quake, the cash register in the basement had been rigged so that periodically a red star would appear on the printed receipt. The mark meant that the purchaser was entitled to another round of drinks, free. On the day of the quake, when the waiter brought Tom Shepherd the martinis he ordered for his birthday, there was a star on his tab.

"Well, look," he had said, "a red star. It never happened before, and on my birthday. This is an earthshaking event." And then the earthquake started.

Michael McGee poses with his daughter Sarah in 1964. Stationed at Elmendorf Air Force Base at the time, McGee, now retired from the Air Force, gives a firsthand account of Alaska's great earthquake. (Courtesy of Michael McGee)

Environments NOW...

Akutan and Mageik Volcanoes Attract Scientists' Attention

Akutan Volcano, on Akutan Island 30 miles northeast of Dutch Harbor, has been letting off steam again. Meanwhile scientists remain puzzled about reports of possible steam emissions from Mount Mageik (muh-GEEK), located in Katmai National Park about 290 miles southwest of Anchorage.

Several pilots observed a small steam plume rising from Akutan Volcano during afternoon and early evening March 8. One pilot reported ash-covered snow on the southwest side of the volcano's crater. The apparently brief period of activity had ended by the next morning.

Residents of nearby Akutan Village, located along the coast 10 miles east of the summit, did not report any signs of volcanic activity. There are no seismometers on Akutan Island, and no plumes were visible on satellite images.

Akutan is one of the most active volcanoes of the Aleutian arc, having erupted at least 27 times since 1790. The last significant eruption was in March and April 1988. Minor steam activity is common at Akutan, and several times a year the activity typically results in minor, local ash emissions such as what occurred in March. Similar activity involving minor ash emission occurred in mid-September 1991.

Unlike Akutan, Mount Mageik has no confirmed history of eruptive activity, although steam often vents from fumaroles near the summit. Alaska Volcano Observatory geologists do not count steam eruptions in their tallies of official eruptive activities. Yet early in the morning March 3, an unusual cloudform appeared on satellite imagery in the vicinity of the young stratovolcano. Efforts by Alaska Volcano Observatory geologists failed to confirm any type of eruption. During flights around and downwind of Mageik, they saw no ash or debris flows. Neither was sulphur dioxide, a volcanogenic gas, detected by monitors on board the aircraft.

The mysterious cloud remained on satellite pictures for several hours as it drifted northeastward at about 20,000 feet elevation. It appeared to dissipate over the Prince William Sound and Copper River Basin areas.

Mount Mageik is located about four miles southwest of Novarupta, the site of a major eruption in 1912. Mageik is also about 1.5 miles southwest of the site of the lava flow and cone-building eruption of the Trident volcanic cluster from 1953 to 1968.

— *From the Alaska Volcano Observatory*

Akutan Volcano, 4,275 feet, erupts steam and ash during October 1978. In March 1992, pilots reported that the volcano was erupting again, with ash-covered snow spotted on the mountain's southwest flank. The volcano, about 30 miles northeast of Dutch Harbor, is among the most active in the Aleutians. (Staff)

Fairbanks' Fort Knox

LEFT: *This view looking south across the rolling hills on the north side of the Tanana Valley shows the Fort Knox exploration and development area about 20 miles northeast of Fairbanks. (Tom Bundtzen)*

BELOW: *Russian and American geologists examine 6-inch-in-diameter drill cores from the Fort Knox project. The large diameter drill core is used to test metallurgical characteristics of the potential ore body and check results of other drilling programs using other drilling methods. (Tom Bundtzen)*

The Fort Knox gold deposit north of Fairbanks appears to be one of the three largest gold finds currently known in the state.

The deposit contains between 3.1 and 4.2 million ounces of proven and probable reserves, ranking it between the Alaska-Juneau deposit of about 4 million ounces and the Kensington deposit near Juneau at about 2.4 million ounces.

The Fort Knox deposit is unusual in its size — at least 125 million tons of low grade ore — and its purity. Fort Knox gold is extremely pure, containing practically no silver. Gold ore normally contains up to 40 percent silver as an admixture alloy.

Formerly known as the "Melba" or "Monte Cristo" prospect, the Fort Knox deposit is a large, potentially bulk-minable gold-bismuth deposit hosted in 90-million-year-old granite. It is located on the north flank of Gilmore Dome, about 20 miles northeast of Fairbanks. Its granite host is another distinguishing feature of the deposit. Most hard rock gold polymetallic veins in the Fairbanks district are in quartz veins in metamorphic schist; mineral occurrences in granite were largely ignored in earlier years.

The deposit was worked on a limited scale in the early part of this century. A small mining machine called a jaw crusher was put in place on the property prior to 1920.

In the mid-1980s, a small company headed by Dan Nye, a prospector and mining consultant from Fairbanks, began to explore the deposit. Work accelerated in 1987 when Fairbanks Gold Ltd. from Vancouver, Canada, bought the property. Two years later, Fairbanks Gold and their previous operator, WGM Inc. of Anchorage, announced that the deposit contained between 3.1 and 4.2 million ounces of gold depending on the "cut off" grade.

Despite some industry skepticism, these estimates have apparently been confirmed by additional work. Since 1987, about $22 million has been spent on the Fort Knox property and seasonal employment levels, mostly exploration crews, have ranged from 45 people to 70 people, according to state records.

In late 1991, AMAX Gold Inc., of Golden, Colo., announced plans to buy the property in a stock transfer worth about $150 million. AMAX executed this transaction, acquired the mineral rights and now the Fort Knox deposit represents about 50 percent of the company's total gold reserves.

AMAX plans to continue development work, conduct environmental assessments and proceed toward production in late 1994 and 1995.

Fort Knox is located on Alaska state lands and could be the first major metal deposit developed on state lands.

—From the Alaska Division of Geological and Geophysical Surveys

LEFT: *This drill works the Fort Knox property during the exploration phase in 1990. (Tom Bundtzen)*

ABOVE: *These sacks are part of a 48-ton bulk sample sent off to metallurgical laboratories in Canada to test for gold recovery and grade parameters. (Tom Bundtzen)*

SHARING

Dear Sirs:

I have borrowed, from the Victoria Public Library, a copy of your *ALASKA GEOGRAPHIC®* entitled *The Upper Yukon Basin.*

It is very interesting to me because my father formed a company, and operated a sternwheel steamer on the upper Yukon River and its tributaries during the Klondike gold rush. It was named the *Prospector.* It was the first steamer ever to navigate the Macmillan River, and then to provide a service to hunters and prospectors there, as well as regular service for freight and passengers on the Stewart, Pelly and the Yukon River between Whitehorse and Dawson.

—(Miss) Edna Meed
Victoria, B.C., Canada

Please send a copy of your Newsletter Index as advertised in Volume 19, Number 1. As a member of your Society for seven to eight years, we have totally enjoyed each issue.

I was stationed at Sitka from October 1942 to April 1943, then in Prince Rupert, B.C. until December 1945, after which we lived in Anchorage from Christmas Day 1945 to May 1951. We have many fond memories of Alaska.

—Eugene J. Scharnek
Milwaukee, Wis.

Northern Ink...

Kusiq, An Eskimo Life History from the Arctic Coast of Alaska, by Waldo Bodfish, Sr.; recorded, compiled and edited by William Schneider; in collaboration with Leona Kisautaq Okakok and James Mumigana Nageak; University of Alaska Press, Fairbanks; 330 pages, 26 black-and-white photos, four maps, bibliography and index, softcover, $21.

In *Kusiq*, Waldo Bodfish Sr. tells a remarkable story of Eskimo life on Alaska's arctic coast. Bodfish, 90, an Inupiat from Wainwright southwest of Barrow, recalls his days as a reindeer herder, hunter, trapper, big-game guide, census taker and as a radio operator for the National Weather Service during World War II.

His story reflects a natural chronology of events from his childhood — he was born in 1902 — to the present. His family herded reindeer, and journeys with the herd took him up and down the coast, from Teller to Point Hope, Icy Cape, Point Lay and Barrow. Bodfish attended school a few years at Teller Mission, headed by Lutheran missionary T.L. Brevig. He tells about his time there, and about seasonal activities, which included summer work at Nome. His family worked on a passenger

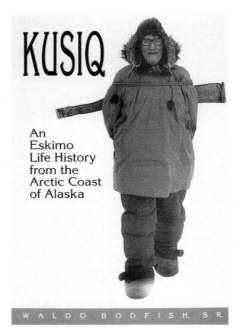

KUSIQ

An Eskimo Life History from the Arctic Coast of Alaska

WALDO BODFISH, SR.

boat that traveled between Teller and Nome, and he earned money running errands. Bodfish recalls his Inupiat teachers, elders who showed him skills needed for survival, like his grandmother Ahnugulook, who sewed squirrel and muskrat parkas and sealskin boots for him and taught him how to snare squirrels. He gives a wonderfully personal account of killing his first seal. His sense of humor comes across in a tale about swimming naked across a river to round up reindeer that had strayed

too far. "When I got to the middle [of the river], a spotted seal pup was alongside of me and scared the heck out of me plenty," he says. "I thought he was going to bite me, but he never touched me. Sometimes he went under me and came up on the other side. I swam across holding on to the reindeer's tail. I didn't have hard work. But I was scared like anything from that spotted seal. I thought he was going to bite on my leg or on my arm or belly." He tells about building ice houses, then the improvement that sod houses brought; about trading with white fur buyers, about traveling by dog-powered umiak up rivers. Readers can hear the eagerness he felt at learning adult skills, the sadness he felt burying his stepfather, and his pride at learning to "herd like any man." While a personal account, Bodfish's lively narrative shows the culture and traditions of the Inupiat people during much of this century, largely before their lives were altered by the discovery of North Slope oil.

Bodfish's first-person account takes up the first 12 chapters, about half the book. The remainder was written by Bodfish's biographer William Schneider, curator of oral history at the Elmer E. Rasmuson Library, University of Alaska

Fairbanks, and collaborators Leona Kisautaq Okakok and James Mumigana Nageak. Their supporting chapters give historical and cultural background, provide context for Bodfish's narrative, and tell about the pleasures and challenges of producing this oral history.

Schneider first met Waldo and his wife, Mattie, in 1978 when he was working for the National Park Service to document historic sites in the Wainwright area. He traveled extensively with Waldo the next two summers, during which time he began to realize how much Waldo had done and seen and the depth of his knowledge. In 1985, Edna Ahgeak MacLean and Schneider conceived the idea of a life history project. MacLean appealed to the North Slope Borough Commission on History, Language and Culture. The commission funded her request. Schneider was completing a life history of Athabaskan Moses Cruikshank and was excited to work with an Inupiat elder. Because of his previous experience with Waldo Bodfish, a keen observer with an excellent memory for detail, Schneider asked Bodfish to share his life story. Bodfish's story, says Schneider, is important to our understanding of North Slope history and culture.

The story that appears in *Kusiq* (Bodfish's Inupiaq name) is a composite edited from 25 hours of taped interviews. Schneider transcribed the tapes into an archival manuscript, a clearly understandable story but one too long and rambling for a general audience. Schneider then edited the text to produce a draft of the published version. He estimates that 80 percent of the original information is contained in this version. "My major considerations in editing the final narrative were to preserve Waldo's style and meaning to facilitate the presentation of his story in written form for a broad audience of students and scholars of the North," Schneider writes in chapter 14, "The Collaborative Process."

A number of people, including Waldo and Mattie, reviewed the draft. Many of the reviewers' comments are included as separate chapters and appendices.

Leona Okakok, deputy director of administration at the planning department of the North Slope Borough, discusses in the book how she worked with Waldo's narrative to determine correct English interpretations and accurate Inupiaq spellings. She offers additional insight into Inupiaq useage and meanings.

James Nageak, instructor of Inupiaq at the Alaska Native Language Center, UAF, accompanied Schneider on the final review of the manuscript with Bodfish. Nageak speaks Waldo's native tongue, and his interview with Bodfish brought out differences in Waldo's storytelling style when he was speaking with someone familiar with hunting and Inupiaq. Park of Nageak's interview with Bodfish is included. Nageak presents a whale-hunting story told to him by Bodfish in Inupiaq, then a literal translation into English, then an edited English translation for a general audience. This exercise highlights the richness of the Inupiaq language. It also illustrates how an interview is shaped by the narrator's perceptions of the listener's background and how translation must go beyond the actual words to the concepts expressed, according to Schneider.

Even noted anthropologist Richard Nelson contributes. After reading a draft, Nelson remarked how little Bodfish had discussed hunting. Nelson writes about the types of hunting stories Bodfish shared with him; Nelson lived in Wainwright when Bodfish was in his 60s. He tells stories about Bodfish as an audacious caribou hunter, braving storms that no one else would venture into. "Waldo was the main person I learned from in terms of intellectual knowledge, traditional knowledge of the past, the kind of knowledge you don't really see when you're out hunting, the kind of thing that's mental," writes Nelson. "I would go over to his house, and bingo! — he would just start talking about these things. He had an inexhaustible capacity for conversation and for storytelling, and a phenomenal memory. So he would just leap off into subjects. I spent a tremendous number of hours in his house, listening."

Schneider also writes a chapter offering a historical context for important periods in Bodfish's life, from early exploration of the arctic coast to the relationship between Bodfish's mother and his father, a successful white whaling captain Hartson Bodfish from New Bedford, Mass. Bodfish was raised by his mother and taught Inupiat skills and customs; he recalls that his father provided material support including groceries during his seasonal visits for whaling. In this chapter, Schneider covers the decline in commercial whaling, provides background on important communities such as Teller, discusses the reindeer industry, World War II and the link to the Outside it brought to the Arctic, pioneer aviators, fur traders and Waldo's Inupiaq teachers.

Schneider wanted Bodfish's narrative to read as if the man was talking in an uninterrupted flow. Although the text is footnoted, these notes are grouped by chapters in the back of the book. This organization suits Schneider's intentions, but flipping back and forth is a bit cumbersome. However, the notes are enlightening and worth the effort to read them along with the story.

Several appendices accompany the text, and black-and-white photos complete this account of life on the North Slope during a time when it was a much more isolated region of our country.

As the Rev. Samuel Simmonds of Barrow writes in the Foreword: "(Waldo) has a unique and interesting way of telling his experiences that allows a person to learn about arctic survival at the same time. As you flip through the pages of this book you will not only enjoy his life stories, but you will also see clearly the passing of the old Eskimo way of life."

—*L.J. Campbell*

PUBLISHED BY
The Alaska Geographic Society

Penny Rennick,
EDITOR

Kathy Doogan,
PRODUCTION DIRECTOR

L.J. Campbell,
STAFF WRITER

Jan Westfall,
MARKETING MANAGER

Kevin Kerns,
CIRCULATION/DATABASE MANAGER

© 1992 by The Alaska Geographic Society